THE AUTHOR

MICHAEL KENT O'LEARY is Assistant Professor of Political Science at the Maxwell School of Citizenship and Public Affairs of Syracuse University. Professor O'Leary was awarded his A.B. by the University of Southern California, and his M.A. and Ph.D. by Princeton University. He has held a Research Fellowship at the Brookings Institution and has taught at Princeton and at Dartmouth College, where he was also Assistant to the Director of the Public Affairs Center. He is the co-author of *Congress in Crisis: Politics and Congressional Reform* and has edited and contributed to *Congressional Reorganization: Problems and Prospects* and *European Views of America: Problems of Communication in the Atlantic World.*

THE POLITICS *of* AMERICAN FOREIGN AID

ATHERTON PRESS · NEW YORK · 1967

THE
POLITICS *of*
AMERICAN
FOREIGN
AID

Michael Kent O'Leary

SYRACUSE UNIVERSITY

FOREWORD BY *Harold Karan Jacobson*

TO THE MEMORY OF MY FATHER

Foreword

HAROLD KARAN JACOBSON *The University of Michigan*

Each year the United States, in full public view, debates its foreign aid program. To start the process, the President submits a budgetary request to the Congress. Usually, his asking figure is not very different from that of the previous year. Congress then considers his request. First an authorization is enacted, and finally the appropriation is granted. At each step the figure is always decreased, sometimes only slightly, at other times significantly. Usually, nearly half a year elapses before the culmination. The public at large may or may not become deeply involved; in no instance, however, is it completely excluded. The debate is inevitably accompanied by some acrimony, and occasionally intense bitterness. Basic aspects of American foreign policy are called into question, and allegations are made that important objectives are being jeopardized. In the end an appropriation has always been enacted, and the aid program continues without interruption. Nevertheless the process is ungain-

ix

ly. It is dismaying not only to the proponents of foreign aid but also to its opponents, albeit for different reasons and to a lesser extent.

American scholars have increasingly been attracted to foreign aid as a subject for analysis, partly because of its importance and intrinsic interest as a basic instrument of modern foreign policy, and partly, no doubt, because they are members of the political system in which the annual appropriation struggle occurs. Generally they have been concerned with the purposes and uses of foreign aid. The understanding of its potentialities and limitations has been improved as a result of scholars' efforts, and, whether they intended it or not, their works have often provided justifications for one or another point of view in the continuing debate. Despite this leavening, the appropriation struggle goes on year after year with little basic change. Even the innovations of a new administration—commissions, study groups, administrative reorganizations—have by now become standard.

Although these scholars have examined various aspects of the appropriating process, no one has systematically analyzed it in its totality. The need for such an analysis is glaringly obvious. Foreign aid is one of the major segments of United States foreign policy, and understanding the way in which funds are appropriated for this purpose is basic to an understanding of how foreign policy is formulated. Moreover, it is conceivable that a better understanding of the process may yield insights as to how it could be improved. Thus an analysis of the subject could benefit both students of and participants in the formulation of foreign policy. Given its obvious utility, such an analysis has been long overdue.

Professor O'Leary's book fills this gap, and with distinction. If overdue, it was well worth the wait. The first comprehensive study of how foreign aid appropriations are made, it is an outstanding piece of work. Starting with an analysis of public opinion and ending with a scrutiny of the role of the executive, it encompasses the entire political system. Its perceptive examination of the entire process is capped with basic and provocative questions about foreign aid and, more broadly, about United States objectives in world affairs. Questions relating to both topics deserve serious debate, and, as Professor O'Leary demonstrates, they ought to be considered together. The book both calls for and significantly contributes to a type of debate on foreign aid that differs substantially from what has occurred in the past.

Even if it did not fill such an important need, the book would deserve commendation for its grace and humor, its obvious scholarship, its skillful blend of quantitative and nonquantitative techniques of analysis. The subject is always the core concern, but every effort is made to provide the most precise and accurate description and analysis possible. The data are handled with skill and imagination. Most importantly, the book deals perceptively with the links among various levels of the political process, a difficult task which few books concerning the formulation of United States foreign policy undertake and fewer still accomplish satisfactorily. The literature on foreign aid contains many separate studies of public opinion, of parties and interest groups, of Congress, and of the Executive, but few have been bold enough to examine the subject in the light of the entire political system. As a consequence, knowledge about the functioning of the system has been curiously uneven. Much is known about how the various parts function, but little about how these parts relate to one another. In this sense, too, Professor O'Leary's treatment is fresh and sorely needed.

I will not foretell the author's findings, nor delay the reader longer. I merely urge the reader on to the study, with my enthusiastic recommendation. I am confident that students of the subject, policy-makers, and interested members of the public alike will find it highly rewarding.

Acknowledgments

In large measure this work is based on documentary research—opinion surveys, government documents, and scholarly works. But at least equal debt is owed to the nearly one hundred participants in the foreign aid policy process who granted interviews which were invaluable in the preparation of this study. Insofar as the pages which follow accurately portray an important arena of American policy-making, the credit is due those who were so generous with their time and knowledge.

At the risk of slighting the many persons who offered helpful advice and criticism, I would like to render individual thanks to four whose contributions were especially valuable: the late Edgar S. Furniss, Jr., who exposed me to the fascination of the politics of foreign policy-making; H. Field Haviland, Jr., who provided shrewd insights into the peripatetic business of research in Washington, D.C.; Stanley Kelley, Jr., who, with firmness tempered by patience and good humor, eliminated some of the manuscript's more glaring errors; and David Baldwin, who further assisted in excising inaccuracies and irrelevancies. Needless to say whatever weaknesses remain are not their fault, but mine.

This study would not have been possible without the disinterested generosity of the Brookings Institution, which enabled me to spend the academic year 1961–1962 in Washington, D.C., as a Research Fellow, and briefer periods after that as a Visiting Scholar to complete the manuscript.

Finally, I am happy to pay tribute to my wife, Judy, whose sharp editorial eye and flagging patience were of substantial assistance in bringing the work to completion.

Contents

THE POLITICS *of* AMERICAN FOREIGN AID

1

Background to Foreign Aid

Many signposts point to America's changing course in world affairs. Among the most striking are Presidential responses to economic hardships abroad. In the 1920s, the nations of Europe were in debt to the United States because of loans made during World War I and were unable to make repayments largely because of American trade restrictions. As they headed toward economic and ultimately political disaster, the American mood was all too well expressed by President Calvin Coolidge, who tartly dismissed suggestions that America render assistance with the observation, "They hired the money, didn't they?" Less than forty years later, President John F. Kennedy voiced a new mood in America's response to the economic plight of peoples abroad when he not only affirmed America's concern but also added a moral commitment: "To those peoples in the huts and villages of half the globe struggling to break the bonds of mass misery, we pledge our best efforts to help them help themselves, for whatever period is required . . . because it is right."

This sharp about-face in American orientation toward world economic problems has, understandably, been accompanied by doubt and criticisms. Yet the trend of policies has been such that when Henry Hazlitt, a severe critic of foreign aid, facetiously asks, "Will dollars save the world?"[1] there is at least a partial reply: The United States Government has in fact become committed to the use of dollars to try to save a world in which Americans can live with freedom and security.

Yet official government commitment is not enough. American foreign aid policy, like many American policies since World War II, operates in a paradoxical context. Officials have at their disposal physical and intellectual resources of a magnitude unprecedented in the history of international relations. These stores of potential power, however, can often accomplish very little by themselves. American officials must, as never before, rely on the cooperation of others—at home and abroad—for the successful conduct of policy. In our concern with what vast and fearful consequences might ensue from the secret decisions of a small handful of officials, we must not lose sight of how current national and international political forces actually restrict the actions of policy-makers.

Foreign aid is a primary case in point. A successful policy requires both technical knowledge to analyze problems and access to the material resources necessary to solve the problems. More than this, assistance programs must be acceptable to those for whom the aid is intended. They must also be actively supported by the American public and Congress. The failure to satisfy this latter requirement, no less than the others, can mean the failure of the entire program.

In the past, governments needed to mobilize widespread public support on foreign policy matters only in times of war. Today, however, if the "long twilight struggle" for economic development is to succeed, it must be constantly supported at every level of American society. The best intentions of policy-makers, the shrewdest analyses of experts, the immense national wealth will

4

be useless if citizens turn against officials who strive to provide assistance abroad, if experts are unwilling to apply their skills overseas, or if Congress will not support the policies.

Any study of foreign aid must come to grips with the difficult problem of definitions. The American government's economic policies range from permitting normal commercial trade, to encouraging trade through various subsidies, to loans with varying terms of repayment, to direct grants. Experts disagree as to where trade leaves off and aid begins. Furthermore, the composition of aid involves everything from surplus food to the skills of technicians, to military, industrial and consumer goods, to direct dollar payments.

Much of the public malaise about foreign aid can be attributed to this ambiguity. Unhappily, a search for the historic origins of foreign aid does not clarify matters. In one sense, America has been in the business of foreign aid for its entire history. When Thomas Paine said, "The cause of America is the cause of all mankind," he expressed a faith that has shaped American thought and action to this day. The American experiment in politics and economics has been judged to be not only for internal use; in the words of Charles Burton Marshall, Americans considered their "new nation . . . an exemplar for all mankind—a nation with a world mission, the guide to a new Jerusalem."[2] Such enthusiasms have transformed trade relations, diplomatic recognition and exchange, and all other political intercourse into opportunities for extending the American way of life as "foreign aid" to willing or unwilling nations.

Much of the "foreign aid" in our early history consisted of admonition and was consequently neither expensive nor effective. At the same time, the American government and people were becoming increasingly engaged in a variety of overseas programs—trade delegations, missionary work, and technical assistance missions —which bear striking, if embryonic, resemblance to more recent activities.[3]

Until just before World War II, there was little explicit government policy to establish precedents for current foreign aid. American actions abroad were the natural, unplanned results of a vigorous and self-assertive society's contacts with the rest of the world. Government's primary contribution came in the years of prewar international crisis when President Franklin Roosevelt embarked on a series of specific, *ad hoc* decisions pointing toward "aid short of war" to the hard-pressed allies. The "destroyers for bases" deal, repeal of the arms embargo, lend lease, and similar measures added a military dimension to American foreign assistance.

The sharp dichotomy in the style of foreign aid— divided between the dispensing of vague, philosophical statements and specific, pragmatic actions in response to foreign threats—was continued after World War II. Although foreign assistance programs multiplied in number and expense, and changed in character, there was scarcely any debate to articulate the implications of a long-range commitment to foreign aid; nothing, for example, comparable to the extensive public and private discussions about establishing the United Nations or stationing troops in Europe during peacetime. From this lack of debate opponents of foreign aid delight in inferring a cunning conspiracy by which the government hoodwinked Americans into accepting foreign aid bit by bit. The fact is, however, that decisions were made rapidly in response to repeated threats, which precluded any long-range public (and most private) discussion.

At the end of World War II the United States was giving assistance to war-torn lands through the United Nations Relief and Rehabilitation Administration (UNRRA) and was planning for long-run cooperation through the International Bank for Reconstruction and Development (IBRD) and the International Monetary Fund. And in 1946, President Truman received authority to loan Great Britain $3.75 billion for reconstruction and relief.

By 1947 the magnitude of the task of rebuilding

Europe, plus the fear of Russian expansion, convinced policy-makers that something more had to be done. The result was the European Recovery Program, more commonly known as the Marshall Plan, after Secretary of State George C. Marshall. As submitted to Congress, the plan called for a four-year program of $17 billion in American grants and loans, which was about 5 per cent of the anticipated total required to rebuild the sixteen countries of Europe. After initial opposition, the plan received the endorsement of both Republicans and Democrats in a degree of bipartisanship unique in the congressional treatment of foreign aid policy.[4]

Even as the Marshall Plan was moving toward a successful conclusion, events outside Europe presented new challenges to thinking about foreign economic assistance. What had been feared in Europe—Communist military advances or the growth of Communist movements within unstable societies—was actually occurring in Korea and China, and was threatening elsewhere in Asia. Responding to these challenges, the Truman administration embarked on still broader foreign military and economic assistance policies, to the Philippines, to Chiang Kai Shek's forces in China, to Korea, and to India. Most significantly, President Truman, in the famous "Point Four" of his inaugural address on January 20, 1949, called upon Americans to look beyond immediate problems, and to "embark on a bold new program" not just to ward off military threat or to compensate for natural disaster, but to promote "improvement and growth of underdeveloped areas."

These two themes—helping others defend themselves against military threat, and cooperating in economic and social development—have continued to serve as the prime justification for the foreign aid policies which have become more or less institutionalized in the late 1960s. The bulk of foreign aid is now approved in a legislative package of military and economic assistance through loans and grants averaging slightly less than $4 billion annually. (During this period, the magnitude has declined from about 2 per cent of the Gross National Product in 1946 to about one-half of one per cent of the GNP in 1966.)

Besides the basic foreign aid program, additional foreign assistance has been rendered through several special channels. The Export-Import Bank, originally established by the Roosevelt Administration as an anti-Depression measure to promote American trade, has come to be considered an aid-giving agency since it makes foreign loans at less than market interest rates. Since 1954, surplus agricultural products have been made available to foreign nations as grants or low-cost sales. In 1961 the Peace Corps was established to make effective use of another kind of "surplus"—American talents and energies for teaching and other tasks to promote growth and development abroad.

The government has also contributed to several multilateral programs—the United Nations, the IBRD and its subsidiary agencies, the International Finance Corporation and the International Development Association, and more recently the Inter-American and Asian Development Banks.[5]

The growing complex of assistance policies has been subjected to careful analysis by scholars and experts from many fields. Economists have addressed themselves to the problems of understanding and defining the process of economic development, and have tried to assess the effectiveness of alternative means of spurring development. Sociologists and anthropologists have investigated the varieties of cultural settings to which assistance programs must conform in order to succeed. Specialists in agriculture, education, public health, public administration, public finance, and many other fields have applied their technical knowledge to the needs and policies of recipient nations. And, somewhat belatedly, political scientists have begun to explore the many questions of international behavior and influence involved in this newly expanded aspect of American foreign policy.

Rather than considering the continuing problems of

implementing aid policy and of evaluating the successes and failures of foreign aid, this book will give
an introspective look at the subject—an examination of
the domestic political process which helps shape American foreign aid policy. The uncertain and often conflicting responses provoked by the issues of foreign aid
have prompted commentators to treat domestic policy-
making decisions with contempt or dismay, or to ignore
them altogether. At best, domestic politics are treated
in an episodic fashion as the interests of the analyst
dictate, with attention directed to a certain congressional
speech favoring or criticizing aid, a particular legislative
decision to raise or lower portions of foreign-aid funds,
or a single speech by a prominent citizen on some question of foreign aid. However, the general and continuing
patterns of public and congressional responses are important for several reasons.

First, the somewhat haphazard political debate over
foreign aid is itself significant, for it reflects the fact
that the practitioners of aid have rarely tried, in public
at least, to establish clearly the temporal, financial, and
political limits of the program. It remains uncertain
whether the notions of the man in the street about
foreign aid are only slightly more hazy than those of the
policy-makers themselves. In any event, the public and
Congress—whether knowledgeable, rational and farsight-
ed, or uninformed, prejudiced, and impatient—have a
vital and inescapable role in helping make the fundamental national decisions as to whether, and to what
degree, the United States should be committed to, and
therefore partly responsible for, economic and social
growth overseas.

This assumption that the public view of foreign aid
is important forms the rationale for the first step in our
investigation of American politics and foreign aid. As
we concern ourselves with the elusive and fascinating
topic of how general traits in the American political
culture condition the perceptions and judgments of broad
elements of the public, we will inquire into the mood of

the public concerning foreign aid.[6] From this starting point, we shall turn to such personal attributes as social background and political beliefs, which have an important bearing on who is for and who against different parts of the foreign aid policies. In our complex society, opinions isolated from politics have little weight; we shall, therefore, also look at those institutions, such as parties and pressure groups, which normally "fix" opinion—in the chemical sense—and channel it to the government in more concentrated forms.

Next we shall consider the essentials of the congressional treatment of foreign aid, concerning ourselves with the question of the extent to which forces motivating the public are also operative in legislative decisions. Finally, we shall examine the executive branch's attempt to win support for its aid policies within the conflicting forces of the American political system.

An overview such as this can necessarily pay but brief attention to each component of the system. The choice of comprehensiveness at the expense of detail has been made with some reluctance, but with a belief that it has some merit. We have already argued that the prime issues of foreign aid are not only technical and external but also philosophical and internal. We are also convinced that these issues are not the preserve of any particular party or faction of the public, or of any one institution of the government, but are so profound and widespread as to constitute a challenge to the comprehension and resolve of the whole nation.

2

Foreign Aid and American

Political Culture

We can best begin to appreciate American thinking about foreign aid by considering the general cultural and ideological environment in which public judgments and evaluations are made. Foreign policy is physically and psychologically remote from most people. Events are so complex and obscure that detailed understanding is beyond the capabilities of all but the expert. As a substitute for sufficient knowledge most people, occasionally even experts, will interpret events in terms analogous to their own experiences, their own traditions, and their own previously established judgments of right and wrong in matters of public policy. We laugh at the sign, "My mind is made up, don't confuse me with facts." Yet this is a slogan we all follow to some degree in making comprehensible an otherwise intolerably complex and uncertain world.[1] We fashion judgments, especially about new policies, on the basis of what we already know and believe.[2]

Our concern with the cultural underpinnings of opinion leads us to expect opinions and attitudes to be formed not so much through deliberate thought and analysis as through reactions to "images" or generalizations about foreign aid. We will investigate, in other words, the affective rather than the effective bases for judgments about foreign aid.[3]

Americans rely on three principal sets of criteria in evaluating foreign aid: whether foreign aid policies are consistent with traditional American responses to the international environment; the role of foreign aid in current diplomatic strategy; and the place of foreign aid in the area of government economic policy.

Internationalism

It has been argued that the sentiment of the American people has historically followed well-defined alternating "moods" in the degree to which internationalist activity is favored.[4] The present is clearly a period of extroversion characterized by an initial presumption in favor of international activity. The frequently described postwar "revolution" in American foreign policy consists in part of public endorsement of increased economic, political, and military activity overseas. In opinion surveys, the public has repeatedly placed questions of war and peace and other international matters at or near the top of the list of the major problems facing this country.[5] Since the last years of World War II, approximately three-fourths of those polled have acknowledged the need for America to take an active role in world affairs.[6]

Approval has also been high for policies of economic assistance abroad. The Marshall Plan enjoyed high levels of support,[7] and even aid for economic development, the more controversial aspect of aid policy, has received more than 60 per cent approval as a *general* proposition.[8] In the press and elsewhere, most public comment presumes the need for some sort of aid, although, as we shall see, there is little consensus as to the details of an optimum foreign aid program.

The exact reasons for this internationalist outlook are not easy to determine, but perhaps a chief factor is the venerable ideal of an American "mission" throughout the rest of the world. This attitude was born in the American Revolution and nurtured in the geographical and economic expansion of the nineteenth century. It reached an aggressive adolescence at the turn of the century and, having attained a somewhat subdued maturity since 1900, it still operates to give strength to the feeling that America can effect an uplifting of the quality of life in foreign nations. Such an attitude does not necessarily imply support for any one type of foreign policy. In some cases the notion of American uniqueness may even lead to a kind of national parochialism calling for exclusion from contacts with the benighted foreigners. But for the most part it helps create support for an activist, even aggressive, style of foreign policy.

The concept of mission has included a strong dose of humanitarianism, a component which lends support to certain forms of foreign aid. The strength of this idealism and humanitarianism can be surprising. On two occasions in 1943 over 80 per cent of survey respondents indicated a willingness to remain on the despised rationing system for another five years, ". . . to help feed the starving people in other countries."[9] In 1959, 73 per cent of poll respondents approved an idea to create a "Great White Fleet" of unused Navy vessels fitted out "as hospital ships, food supply ships, training schools and the like" for the benefit of poorer nations.[10] In March 1966, 61 per cent of a survey named building hospitals, training nurses and doctors, and providing medicine as the kinds of foreign aid which they favored most.[11]

Coupled with humanitarianism as a motivating force in the American missionary ideal is the belief that the "American way of life"—however variously that may be defined—can be exported to the advantage of other nations. This feeling, based on America's self image as "a unique combination of economic power, intellectual and practical genius, and moral rigor,"[12] has contributed

13

important, if selective, support for aid programs. It has helped lead to the high popularity of those aspects of foreign aid which involve Americans in face-to-face relations with foreigners for purposes of teaching, training, and instructing. Such a feeling helps explain the results of the 1966 poll cited earlier, in which between 61 and 65 per cent of the survey favored aid programs in the fields of education and agriculture assistance.[13] This feeling has meant continuing public support for the Point Four technical assistance component of foreign aid which was more popular, in the view of at least one government official, than even the Marshall Plan.[14]

More recently, the American dedication to spreading Americanism has led to enthusiastic support for the Peace Corps.[15] Popular approval is due in large measure to the Peace Corps' image as a means of sending abroad a host of selfless Americans to work with backward peoples and thereby, in the phrase of Sargent Shriver, the Peace Corps' first director, to "energize" activity in the host country.[16] The Peace Corps also profits from the attraction of citizen diplomacy, which has always been at least a minor theme of the patriotic missionary ideal. Indeed, the two-year limit on the tour of Peace Corps volunteers (with a slightly longer limit for the staff) is an echo from the diplomatic style of a much earlier day, when the tenets of Jacksonian democracy called for tenure of about two years in all diplomatic posts.[17]

As we look closely at the characteristics of the American missionary spirit we can see that it contains the seeds of its own negation. If most Americans, as Geoffrey Gorer has argued, consider that taking part in an international undertaking means simply "extending American activities outside the boundaries of the United States,"[18] it follows that foreigners are often expected to reciprocate with appropriately compliant behavior.

Most Americans can scarcely be said to apply close analysis to the detailed consequences of aid policy. But there is evidence that many Americans nevertheless share a general expectation that foreign aid will help "sell" or transmit Americanism abroad. In 1949 the National Opinion Research Center asked a sample of the population whether they thought foreign aid helped the United States. Those who considered aid helpful (55 per cent of the sample) were then asked to give the reasons for their opinions. Of this group, just under half gave answers classifiable as "helps us politically," which seemed to mean either that aid would make others like the United States more, or that it would make them more like the United States: "builds good will, promotes friendly feelings toward us"; "they'll be on our side in case of war"; "it's good propaganda for democracy, capitalism."[19]

Hans Morgenthau has noted the similarity between Wilsonianism and present-day thinking about foreign aid:

> Wilson wanted to bring the peace and order of America to the rest of the world by exporting America's democratic institutions. His contemporary heirs want to bring the wealth and prosperity of America to the rest of the world through the export of American capital and technology.[20]

We might amend this to say that many of his contemporary heirs want to outdo Wilson by exporting political *and* economic institutions through foreign aid.[21]

It should be easy to see how undependable is the support for foreign aid which flows from the missionary spirit. Only frustration and disappointment can result from expectations that aid recipients will mesh their foreign policy with America's, will come to resemble America in their political, economic, and social systems, or even will feel more favorably disposed to America as their benefactor.

Indications of public sensitivity to inadequate foreign responses are not difficult to find. As far back as the late 1940s, when public support for the Marshall Plan was running between 56 per cent and 73 per cent of those interviewed, the NORC uncovered a strong

15

undercurrent of something less than enthusiasm over Europe's own part in the recovery program. On two occasions (December 1947 and April 1949) respondents were asked whether they thought Europeans were working as hard as they could, or whether they were depending too much on the United States for help. It was felt by 64 per cent and 58 per cent of those answering, respectively, that the Europeans were overdependent on the United States.[22] Even earlier soundings of opinion had discovered the same sort of feeling. In October 1945, respondents were asked a two-part question: Should loans for recovery be made to our three wartime allies—England, Russia, and China? If loans were made, would the countries repay them? The replies demonstrated two things about public feeling: the chances for repayment were thought to be rather slim; and sentiment in favor of such a loan to each country varied with the expectation that the country would repay, with China receiving the most favored public judgment (see Table II-1).

Table II-1. PUBLIC OPINION CONCERNING LOANS TO ENGLAND, RUSSIA, AND CHINA

	Expectation that a loan would be repaid		*Agreement that such a loan should be made*
	IN FULL	IN PART	
England	9%	36%	33%
Russia	24	34	40
China	33	34	63

Source: NORC, p. 3.

The negative side of America's response to international aid was illustrated in 1949 by a poll in which those who opposed aid to underdeveloped countries were asked to give their reasons. Over 50 per cent indicated a fear that the psychological rewards of aid would be insufficient—that the recipients would not be grateful, or that aid was in itself inconsistent with American traditions of self-help and minding one's own business.[23]

A more recent example shows how this belief in a unique American mission works both for and against foreign aid. In 1961 there was a brief period of public discussion concerning the desirability of assisting the Ghanian government to build a hydroelectric dam on the Volta River. Most of this discussion, both favorable and unfavorable, was concerned scarcely at all with the economic or technical feasibility of the project. Instead, concern was expressed about the degree of democracy or dictatorship existing at the time in Ghana, and about the extent to which President Nkrumah was favorably disposed toward the Communist Bloc. Those who favored the project argued that American aid would make Ghana's politics more free and stable. Many were opposed because they wondered, with the *Philadelphia Inquirer,* if nations anywhere would see an advantage "in practicing the principles of democracy and freedom, and supporting the fight against communism," since we would be giving money to a government which did neither of these things.[24]

There is a final point about the twofold impact which the American missionary attitude has upon the support of foreign aid. Negative feelings represent much more than simply a diminution of the base for positive reactions. As an aid program departs from those characteristics which make it appear to be essentially American life transplanted abroad, the idealism becomes dampened and the missionary feeling may turn inward, rejecting foreign aid. The workings of this anti-aid syndrome can be easily summarized: Americans tend to assume that other nations want the essence of our political and economic institutions, and that they have the means to obtain them. When this anticipated "universal aspiration toward Americanism"[25] is not manifested in the nations that we help, American fears of being rejected and exploited can lead to an abandonment of international cooperation. Every deviation from American policy goals, every unfriendly gesture by Latin Americans, Africans, or Asians, becomes new justification for cutting down or

17

eliminating aid.[26] As Gorer has summed up this attitude, "People so perverse as to choose to remain foreign deserve no help."[27]

Foreign Aid and Diplomacy

A second major aspect of opinion revolves around consideration of foreign aid's role in American diplomatic strategy, especially in cold-war competition with China and the Soviet Union.

Foreign aid gains support insofar as it is seen as a potent anti-Communist weapon, improving the living standards of others to make them less susceptible to communism, and as an inducement or reward for nations allying themselves with the United States against immediate or potential Communist aggression. Support for the Marshall Plan can be traced in large measure to the widespread feeling not only that American aid to Europe would help prevent the spread of communism by external aggression in Europe but also that in the absence of aid some of the domestic politics of countries would probably become dominated by Communists.[28]

The image of aid as a direct anti-Communist tool has also led to support for military assistance. A series of polls since June 1950 has shown that 60 per cent or more of the population has supported the general notion of military assistance to European and Asian allies.[29] As we shall see later, however, Americans have their doubts about military aid, too.

The view of aid as a diplomatic tool likewise fails to evoke unmixed support. The widespread simplifications involved in opinion-formation are nowhere more apparent than in the case of diplomatic strategy. If aid is to be supported as a tool against international communism, it therefore must not be used ambiguously. Thus, assistance to Communist countries, or even neutrals, is highly inconsistent with the general attitudes favoring aid.

This uncertainty or even antipathy toward aid to

non-allies was clearly shown in a series of 1956 polls which asked whether we should continue to aid "some countries like India, which have *not* joined us as allies against the Communists." The expressed sentiment was as much as 43-50 per cent against continuing such aid.[30]

The American approach to foreign policy commonly distrusts any sharp and basic disagreement with America's conception of world affairs, and includes an active sensitivity to being rejected or exploited by others. This is part of the reason for the extreme bitterness of newspaper and other public reaction to India's military seizure of the Portuguese territory of Goa in 1961. This action was interpreted as an anti-Western and anti-American move just a short time after Prime Minister Nehru, who had received much aid from the United States, had visited this country and had received considerable editorial sympathy.

Another reason for the difficulty of reconciling the concept of aid as a means of advancing the national interest with the policy of aid to nations which do not share American purposes is the unwillingness of the American public to accept the uncertainty of diplomacy —the persistence of its problems and the tentativeness of its opportunities. In arguing as to who should receive aid, public judgments tend toward polar extremes: if a Sukarno or an Nkrumah initiate anti-American actions, they are impossible to deal with and wholly undeserving of aid. If they make the slightest friendly gesture or, better yet, if they are overthrown, then things look much rosier in that region of the world, and the foreign aid gamble is held to be justified.[31] The basic problem remains much the same now as when de Tocqueville, in his study of America, noted that democracy appeared "better adapted for the conduct of society in times of peace, or for a sudden effort of remarkable vigor, than for the prolonged endurance of the great [international] storms that beset the political existence of nations."[32]

For whatever reasons, the American has typically reacted in extremes to foreign policy challenges. He

19

tends to wish to solve international problems by either unentangling precept or short-term massive intervention. This approach is applied to foreign aid as well as other foreign policies. In 1949, when sentiment was 70 per cent or more in favor of aid to underdeveloped countries, a sample of those who approved was asked if the United States should "put up some of the money for this purpose" or "just help in other ways." The division was even (46–46 per cent) between those who were willing to expend money for this purpose and those who selected the unspecified "other ways," which probably seemed less costly and less entangling.[33]

When the choice has been between economic and military aid the pattern has been similar, though more complex. Between June 1948 and December 1952, the NORC conducted seventeen polls which included questions regarding economic aid. Favorable opinion averaged 62 per cent.[34] During approximately the same period (April 1948 through June 1950) a series of questions was asked regarding military aid. Support was about ten points lower, averaging 53 per cent.[35] Similarly, on seven occasions in the 1950s, respondents were asked direct questions as to which they would prefer sending, military or economic aid. In every case economic aid was preferred over military, by margins averaging 36 per cent.[36] On the other hand, after the outbreak of the Korean War support for military aid was much higher. From July 1950 to November 1956 support for military assistance averaged 70 per cent in a series of twelve questions.[37]

In early 1966 a survey showed that the more entangling forms of aid—military assistance, road building, and assistance for capital projects such as factories— were the least popular forms of aid. These forms were chosen by an average of 24 per cent, as opposed to the most popular item, educational assistance, which was chosen by 64 per cent.[38] We are a task-oriented society, and will favor even hazardous and expensive actions if they are measurably achieving some goal. But in the absence of clear-cut goals and achievements, we are likely to limit our risks as much as possible. As V. O. Key concluded, we show a strange mixture of verbal toughness and "of the trustfulness of a delighted puppy when treated in a friendly manner."[39]

The increase in support for military assistance after the outbreak of the Korean War was not simply a shift from pacifism to blind militarism, but rather a change in the interpretation of the international situation. Previously, secondary means were thought sufficient to meet the demands of the international situation; later, both the wealth and the armed force of the United States were seen as necessary to eliminate a state of affairs intolerable because of its threat and ambiguity. It must be remembered that this proposed military assistance which received increased support was not for Asia, where fighting was taking place, but for Europe, where the need for the military was only potential.

The tendency to react in extremes can also be seen in the continuing public debate concerning aid to Communist countries such as Poland and Yugoslavia. Opponents of such aid base their case on the assertion that Poland and Yugoslavia still remain anti-American and pro-Russian in so many respects as to make them unqualified to receive our aid. Those favoring aid do so on the grounds that in the absence of our aid all is lost and that Yugoslav and Polish leaders will be forced to "go all the way back to Moscow."[40]

We can, in other words, speak of a widespread failure to appreciate that both the gains and the losses of diplomacy often are limited and temporary. Americans overestimate both the impact that aid can have on a given international situation and also the degree of change that can be expected during any short period. This trait has been well summarized by the economist Robert Asher, who has spoken of the American tendency:

to oversimplify our problems . . . , to shortcut our way to a solution. One year it's the Bretton Woods agreement that will solve our postwar economic problems; another year it's the Marshall Plan; then it's technical assistance; today [July 1953] it's "trade not aid." We tend to overwork these slogans and, in doing so, to blind ourselves to the complexity and the long-range character of our foreign-economic problems.[41]

Foreign Aid As an Economic Question

Foreign aid, being to a large extent an economic policy, is also judged in terms of economic assumptions and doctrines. As already noted, some of the support which aid has received comes from the belief in the efficacy of a kind of international "full belly" policy as a barrier to the growth of communism within nations. The polls indicate that Americans associate high living standards in both Europe and Asia with low levels of communism.[42]

Economic development has been favored not only as an anti-Communist device, but also as one way in which America could export the economic aspects of Americanism—a healthy, affluent, and, most especially, free enterprise economic system. The passage of time has shown how radically this goal differs from what is, in fact, achievable. Anticipation of widespread imitation of American economic practices no longer serves to back up support for foreign aid.[43]

Polls in the 1940s show support for aid on the basis of more narrowly conceived economic considerations. In the last year of World War II, 78 per cent of respondents agreed with the proposition that "we'll have the best chance of having prosperity in this country by helping other countries in the world get back on their feet . . ."; and 57 per cent agreed that "if our government keeps on sending lend-lease materials, which we may not get paid for, to friendly countries for about three years after the war . . . this will mean more jobs . . . for most Americans. . . ."[44] In response to open-end questions on reasons for liking the Marshall Plan after it was under way,

44 per cent of respondents who favored the Plan volunteered their expectation that it would help the United States economically.[45]

Although, as we shall see in subsequent chapters, arguments are still made in behalf of foreign aid on the basis of its favorable impact on the American economy, such arguments are now sharply challenged. It may very well be that one of the most potent arguments against foreign aid is now the economic one, in particular that aid is too expensive.[46]

It must be pointed out that opposition to aid on the basis of cost, while important, is a secondary phenomenon. The American citizen will support the spending of his tax dollars for many different reasons—altruism, national emergency, or narrow and immediate self-interest. In the philosophical limbo in which foreign aid finds itself, no consistent clear-cut rationale has been advanced to convince any large numbers of people of the wisdom of spending several billions of dollars a year for aid.

The relative saliency of anti-foreign-aid opinions within the context of cost was demonstrated in a 1959 Gallup Poll which asked whether it was preferable to cut back on government spending or to increase taxes. To this vague proposition an unsurprising 72 per cent chose cutting back on spending. This group was then asked what things they would like to see cut back. Of a long list of activities considered expendable, foreign aid was mentioned most frequently—in 30 per cent of the cases, twice as much as the second-place item.[47] A 1949 NORC poll found that the single most frequently mentioned objection to foreign aid was the cost—especially the problems of "sending money overseas" when things needed to be done at home.[48] A 1965 survey found that three times as many people feel we are giving too much aid as feel we are not giving enough.[49]

The anti-spending component of negative attitudes about foreign aid has continued to be rather consistent over time, and is apparently independent of the changing currents of political debate. In 1959, for example, the question of whether to raise or lower the defense budget was being hotly debated in Washington. The Gallup Poll, in order to find out what the public was thinking about this issue, asked respondents to note the budget items for which they thought the government should spend more or less money. In the list of things for which the government should decrease spending, defense was in third place, named by 9 per cent of respondents; leading this list was foreign aid, named by 17 per cent.[50]

On the other hand, when respondents are asked open-end questions about governmental problems *not* in the context of spending, foreign aid does not invoke the same high degree of negative response. In December 1959 the Gallup Poll asked respondents what topics they would like to discuss in letters to their congressmen. Cutting taxes (named by 14 per cent) and labor legislation (named by 10 per cent) headed this list—after the 18 per cent who knew of nothing to write. Opposition to foreign aid was far down the list, mentioned by only 2 per cent.[51]

Interrelationships of Opinion

We can now inquire about the impact on public opinion of the many contrasting images of foreign aid which might activate conflicting attitudes of the man in the street: exporting the American way of life vs. dangerous and uncertain international involvement; worthy assistance to people in need vs. undesirable governmental spending; building bulwarks against communism vs. helping nations which may seem all too friendly to communism.

Some notion of current judgments of aid may be gained from a Gallup Poll of early 1966: "In general, how do you feel about foreign aid, are you for it or against it?" A bare majority, 53 per cent, were in favor of foreign aid, 35 per cent were against it, and 12 per

cent had no or uncertain opinions.[52] Earlier polls show
about the same distribution of opinion, indicating the
persistence of general opinion patterns.[53] This consistency
of the general response, coupled with the wide swings
in responses to variously worded questions, takes us
back to the primary point of this chapter. Foreign aid
means many things, some favored and some feared. To
appreciate public judgments more fully, we need to ask
not only what factors influence opinion about aid, but
also what their relative strengths are.

To begin with, aid benefits simply from being an
internationalist policy. Some additional characteristics
of aid which increase its public approval are: programs
which seem to export elements of American society and
values (ideological aid); programs which contain elements of humanitarianism; programs which support international allies; programs which involve few foreign
entanglements; and programs which are low in cost.
Conversely, other qualities of aid programs increase the
likelihood of opposition: programs which aid nations
that do not share the United States' view of the cold war;
programs which involve relatively deep entanglement in
international problems; and programs which are costly.

Predictably, positive characteristics appearing together in an aid program intensify support, while combinations of negative characteristics intensify opposition.
The Marshall Plan was directed toward a group of familiar countries which increasingly came to be thought
of as allies vis-à-vis the Communist world; Marshall aid
also had a more or less definite price tag and fairly
well-defined goals and time limit. Aid to underdeveloped
nations, on the other hand, is directed toward a host of
unfamiliar peoples and societies whose international loy-
alties are uncertain at best, and is of open-ended cost,
uncertain ends, and indefinite duration.

Specific poll questions bear this out. In 1955 and
1956 the NORC asked a series of questions concerning
economic aid. These questions sought opinion on the
economic, and therefore relatively unentangling, form

of aid and also aid to "countries that have agreed to stand with us against Communist aggression," thereby stressing two of the positive factors mentioned above. The average rate of approval for this type of aid was 83 per cent. At the same time the respondents were asked about giving economic aid to "countries like India, which have *not* joined us as allies against the Communists." The average approval of this proposition—a desirable type of aid to non-allies—was only 49 per cent.[54]

Similar evidence of the interaction of positive and negative factors can be found in public comment on policies of giving food to people in Communist countries. Opinion seems to be divided about evenly. Some, even among those who generally oppose aid to Communist countries, say we should not use starvation as a weapon. Others reply that sending food to starving peoples in Communist countries is doing them no favor if it helps strengthen their oppressive governments.[55]

It appears that the elements affecting evaluations of foreign aid may be tightly compartmentalized in the public mind. It will be recalled that in one previously cited poll only 33 per cent of respondents approved of a loan to England when they were asked about it within the context of the cost, through a preliminary inquiry into whether or not the loan would be repaid. In the same poll 82 per cent agreed that "the United States should continue to give relief to the people in European countries that were occupied by the enemy—such as France and Greece."[56] It is possible, of course, that the sharp difference in answers to these two questions is a result of strong anti-British and pro-French and Greek feeling by the sample interviewed. But it seems more reasonable to account for these differences by the wording of the questions, one stressing the strong negative factors of cost and possible non-repayment; the other stressing a positive factor—humanitarian assistance.

This compartmentalized thought also occurs in relation to other aspects of opinion about foreign aid. In an investigation of the relationship between opinions on cutting taxes and on supporting foreign aid, V. O. Key found that only one-fifth of those he studied "maintained a consistent position on both issues. . . . It may be that only about one-fifth of the population can be relied upon to give a consistently sensible and firm support to interrelated policies of the kinds described."[57]

Weighing Positive and Negative Factors

What are the relative weights of these positive and negative factors, or their ability to influence opinion in one direction or another?

Some of the polling on foreign aid is helpful in this process. Many poll questions are worded in such a way as to elicit opinion about different kinds of aid. By comparing responses to poll questions on different aspects of the aid program we can make inferences about the relative popularity or unpopularity of various kinds of aid. We can make such comparisons most effectively when two conditions prevail: (1) A given question pertains to two factors on which opinion seems to be based; (2) A set of two or more such questions has one factor in common. We compare, for example, the responses to a question regarding ideological-type aid to neutrals with responses to a question regarding humanitarian aid to neutrals in order to determine the ranking of the missionary and humanitarian factors. (See the Appendix for a discussion of this complete process.)

Through this method we have obtained the rankings of four of the positive factors and three of the negative. In the order of their ability to provoke a favorable response, the positive factors are: ideological aid, humanitarianism and low involvement (of equal weight), and aiding allies. The negative factors, in order of their importance in influencing a negative response, are: aid to neutrals or non-allies, high cost, and deep involvement.

The importance ascribed to ideological missionary feelings is to some extent borne out empirically since this style of aid tends to rank not only as the strongest positive factor but also as more influential than any of the three negative factors listed. Also, the factors which can logically be paired—aid to allies and aid to non-allies, low involvement and great involvement—do not have equal weight. The positive influence exerted by aid to allies is less strong than the negative influence of aid to non-allies. And low involvement is stronger than its negative equivalent.

Thus, an aid program which gave assistance to allies and non-allies would tend to lack public support. Key's research has given indirect support to this point. Opinions opposing aid to neutrals (non-allies) are held with an intensity more than two and one-half times greater than opinions favoring such aid.[58]

Similarly, if one segment of the population saw an aid program as requiring deep involvement while an equal segment saw it as requiring little involvement, the program would benefit in terms of popular support.

The reasons for these uneven rankings are not always clear. In the case of aid to allies vs. non-allies, asymmetry may result from the general association of allies with the negative concepts of deep involvement and possible high cost. In the same way the negative strength of deep involvement may be weakened by its tendency to be associated with either missionary or humanitarian activities.

The analysis also shows, however, that these factors cannot be given even ordinal rankings which hold in every case. A "humanitarian, aid to allies" question and a "humanitarian, high cost" question, for example, have the same level of public approval. This presents a paradox in formal logic but not necessarily in social psychology. It seems reasonable for a strongly held factor such as humanitarianism either to cancel out negative factors with which it is associated or to make accompanying positive factors irrelevant.

3

The Political Distribution of Opinion

We can make politically relevant inferences from public opinion only when we discover something about how opinions are distributed throughout the political system. Opinions may be widely dispersed or concentrated in geographic regions; they may be held by active or inactive groups; and the issues which parties and candidates choose to emphasize make some opinions more important than others. For these reasons and others a given distribution of opinion may have widely differing kinds of impact on policy-making.

But exact conclusions about policy-making are seldom arrived at from the knowledge of opinion distribution alone. We have only imperfect knowledge of both the balance of opinion on a particular set of issues and of the workings of the American political system. The most we can hope to discover is the nature of the raw materials available to officials in fashioning acceptable policies.

The rather simple conclusion which will serve as a theme in this chapter's discussion is: relevant opinion is distributed throughout the population in such a way that almost equal weight is given to the proponents and opponents of American foreign aid policy. The nearly even division of general opinion noted in Chapter 2 is merely one gross indication of a division of influence in which neither proponents nor opponents of aid enjoy significant political advantages. We shall observe this theme in four contexts: the geographical distribution of opinion; the relationship between opinion and socio-economic groupings; the relationship between opinion about foreign aid and other political opinions; and pressure-group behavior arising out of the distribution of opinion.

Geographic Distribution of Opinion

Geographical distributions of opinion have concerned students of public opinion since the beginning of the United States. On some foreign policy issues geographical location has been an important determinant. Many early political clashes on foreign policy revolved around the difference between Westerners, who saw protection of navigation rights on the Mississippi as the prime national interest, and New Englanders, who placed a higher value on fishing and shipping rights in the Atlantic.[1] At other times regionalism has only referred to geographically-grouped opinions about nonregional matters; location per se has not been so important. Midwestern isolationism before World War II is one example. In certain imaginative explanations, isolationism was said to be caused by the insularity of people in the region. More thorough analysts have pointed out, however, that the Midwest was the home of large numbers of German-Americans who were anti-British and quite unreceptive to the anti-German policies implied by intervention in the 1930s.[2] But whether it is a primary or secondary matter, regional differences are always worth considering, for geographically concentrated opinions frequently have greater political impact than those which are diffuse. When we speak of "strategic minorities" in American politics, we often mean nationwide minorities which are concentrated in states or congressional districts in such a way that they are assured of representation and influence in government far beyond their numbers.

In the case of foreign aid, geographical division of opinion shows two chief characteristics. The first is a generally high incidence in all areas of the most basic factor favoring aid—internationalism. Poll results cited by Key show that internationalism is generally high in all areas of the United States.[3] Furthermore, the pattern of general support also prevails for specific foreign aid programs. The Peace Corps, which had a nationwide approval level of 71 per cent, received high approval in all seven geographical regions used by the Gallup Poll. Only one region (the Pacific), with a figure of 65 per cent, deviated by as much as six percentage points from the average.[4]

From another viewpoint, the distribution of opinion is more complex. In the first place, simple internationalism may serve to support many different kinds of foreign policies. One characteristic of the so-called "conservative isolationism" or "new nationalism" is the desire for increased foreign involvements; it is the nature of the involvement desired—immediate, concrete action directed toward unambiguous goals—which distinguishes opposing groups.[5] In Max Lerner's aphorism, "Prick the skin of a go-it-aloner and you draw interventionist blood. . . ."[6] Such opinions are unlikely to provide support for very many kinds of foreign aid programs. The South, the center of much militant "new isolationism,"[7] has the lowest percentage of poll respondents saying they approved of foreign aid in general. As compared to a nationwide average of 51 per cent, the South had only 38 per cent in favor of foreign aid.[8]

The widespread hostility of the South to foreign aid is especially interesting in light of the historical internationalism of the region. A series of domestic and international developments has converged to create for the Southerners a set of attitudes sharply unfriendly to economic aid to other nations. Military aid represents the kind of direct-action opposition to communism favored in the South. Aid of a clear missionary character is also viewed favorably.[9] But most foreign aid taps images and invokes analogies to which the Southerner has come to be aggressively hostile. Alfred Hero, a leading student of Southern attitudes, has pointed out that things could have been different. Southerners have come to look upon themselves as victims—almost colonial peoples—in a hostile United States. They might have transferred this feeling into sympathy for other colonies and post-colonial peoples throughout the world, appreciating their aspirations for self-determination and material development. But this was not to be. Foreign aid has come to be seen as a costly enterprise, and Southerners take second place to none in their opposition to federal spending.[10] Much foreign aid is directed toward the kind of ambiguous foreign policy actions which Southerners find incomprehensible. And, of course, the race issue has molded opinions on foreign aid as it has opinions on most subjects. It has done so in at least two ways. First, foreign aid means helping colored peoples and colored leaders abroad—a task hardly appealing to the inhabitants of a region accustomed to dealing with the Negro in a position of subordination. And as the federal government has increasingly taken steps to prevent deprivation and harassment of Negroes, all its policies have come to be opposed by Southerners; the general vulnerability of foreign aid is thus intensified.[11]

The possibilities for stalemate inherent in the distribution of opinion can be briefly indicated at this point by considering the legislative representation from various geographical regions. Those states with the lowest general approval of foreign aid (44 per cent in a 1958 Gallup Poll) sent to the Congress 57 per cent of the members of the House of Representatives and 52 per cent of the Senators.[12] There is not a perfect correlation between opinions and votes in Congress. But opinion has some influence; in this case a nationwide minority opposing aid is represented by a majority in each house of Congress.

Opinion and Socioeconomic Background

Two critical variables in assessing the political significance of opinion are the intensity with which opinions are held, and the extent to which opinion holders are likely to act in backing up their beliefs. Intensity is a psychological variable; the likelihood of action is a social characteristic only partly related to intensity. But from the policy-maker's viewpoint, the two are closely connected. Effective public opinion is that which, for whatever reason, is backed up with action. From a policy viewpoint it may not matter whether the action is motivated by intense opinions among those not normally active, or by moderately held opinions among groups which are generally active in giving political support to their views.

There is little direct evidence available concerning the intensity with which favorable opinions are held. We can, nevertheless, make some inferences about this important variable.

Favorable opinion on foreign aid is strongly related to high levels of education. Approval increases so that supporting opinions in excess of 60 per cent are found among the mere 17 per cent of the population who have at least a partial college education. Similarly, classifying responses by occupation shows that favorable responses of 60 per cent or more are found among three groups (professional, executive, and sales), which constitute only 29 per cent of the American working population.[13]

A 1956 Gallup Poll, in asking whether Congress should continue the $4 billion foreign-aid appropriations, recorded not only "Yes" and "No" responses, but the number of respondents who hedged their "Yes" and "No" answers with some qualifications. We will assume that

a low percentage of qualified answers and a low percentage of "No opinion" responses indicate high opinion
intensity. When these figures are computed according
to occupational categories, the results show that 30 per
cent of both the strongest supporters of aid (professionals, executives, and sales personnel) and the remaining
pro-aid group qualified their "Yes" response. The occupational categories most opposed to aid also had 30
per cent of qualified "No" answers. Among those who
answered "No" in the three highly pro-aid groups, however, 43 per cent gave some qualifications to their negative response. Furthermore, professionals, executives, and
sales people averaged only 4 per cent without opinions
as opposed to 14 per cent for the other groups. In other
words, while the two groups had equal proportions of
members giving qualified pro-aid responses, the group
more favorable to foreign aid contained relatively fewer
members with no opinions and relatively more members
whose anti-aid response was given with some qualifications.[14]

The suggested pattern of a relatively small minority
holding strongly to a set of ideas regarding which the
majority is apathetic or antagonistic is supplemented by
reference to data on political participation. The educational and occupational groups found to have the highest
incidence of support for foreign aid are also the ones
most active in the field of politics,[15] a characteristic
which would seem to qualify as a functional equivalent
for intensity. Even if the pro-aid and anti-aid groups
had similar intensities of opinion, we should be alert to
the probability that the three white-collar groups would
be more active in trying to advance their beliefs. The
pattern of stalemate is reinforced by recalling Key's
findings that some anti-aid opinions are held with greater
intensity than some pro-aid sentiment.

The possibilities for stalemate can also be seen in
the relative concern about foreign aid among groups
with different levels of education. We have already
noted that when respondents were asked for their opin-

ion on aid, support increased as we moved from less to more education. However, when respondents in another poll were asked to volunteer those items of government spending they would most like to see reduced, respondents having the least and those having the most education mentioned foreign aid with nearly the same frequency—22 and 29 per cent respectively. Those whose lack of education would lead one to expect from them more frequent mention of cutting foreign aid did not do so because the issue was not prominent in their thoughts; those with more education tended not to mention reducing aid because of a generally favorable opinion. Those in a middle position educationally (having partially completed high school) considered foreign aid expendable by a significantly larger amount, 40 per cent, than those with either more or less schooling. The figures are: 0–8 years of education, 22 per cent; high school, incomplete, 40 per cent; high school graduates or greater, 29 per cent.[16] Clearly, a little learning is a dangerous thing for support of foreign aid.

Foreign Aid and Partisan Politics

When, as with foreign aid, opinions do not constitute a consensus, the institutions which link opinion with government take on great potential importance. Of special interest are the roles of parties and elections. The treatment of foreign aid and foreign policy during the 1960 and 1964 Presidential campaigns can illuminate some of the relationships between elections and the foreign aid policy-making process. We shall devote most of our attention to the 1960 campaign since it is especially relevant to our purposes. It was a close election, conducted by two candidates seeking electoral support from many of the same groups, although they frequently appealed for support in quite different fashion.

The campaign between Lyndon Johnson and Barry Goldwater is less illuminating, and less typical of recent

American Presidential elections. In 1964 Goldwater en-
thusiastically advocated a hard-line foreign policy, abandoning the position of moderate to President Johnson,
who could content himself with the most general defense
of assistance to underdeveloped countries. Foreign aid,
in Goldwater's strategy, was of little consequence. His
idea of desirable foreign aid was limited almost exclusively to what we earlier termed ideological aid and
assistance to cold-war allies. On the whole, Goldwater
seemed to have been relatively uninformed on the subject. In 1960 Goldwater had opposed American aid, giving
as his reason a professed ignorance of any Soviet assistance to underdeveloped nations. This was, as a Republican colleague reminded him, several years after the
Soviets had, among other things, begun to help Egypt
build the Aswan Dam.[17]

The 1960 campaign offers more material for analysis.
Observers have noted the abundance of foreign policy
arguments presented during that campaign; both Richard
Nixon and John F. Kennedy stressed that on the results
of the election hinged the supremely important question
of America's place in the world. Indexes of the two
candidates' speeches contain page after page of references to foreign countries, from Afghanistan to Yugoslavia, and foreign policy issues, from Ambassadors to
the World Bank.[18] Despite the quantity of talk about foreign policy, however, the two candidates in fact treated
it as a secondary issue, employing the vocabulary of
foreign relations merely to help weave their basic campaign appeals, the "plot in which the candidate can play
the hero."[19]

This anomaly arises in part from the strategies candidates employ in presenting campaign issues. Essentially,
there are two alternative methods of dealing with issues.
Candidates may offer policy choices to the electorate as,
for example, more or less social welfare policies, a more
or less progressive tax structure, and more or less activity
in a certain foreign policy endeavor. This involves defending a position, reinforcing the committed, and con-

verting the undecided. Candidates may, on the other hand, try to assess the existing views of voters in order to wage campaigns which associate themselves with voters' preferences and associate their opponents with things disliked by voters. Associating incumbents with corruption in government, connecting Democrats with the Korean War, and bracketing the Republicans with the Depression are examples of this second approach to the presentation of issues.[20]

To the extent that the first method—exposition and advocacy of a possibly controversial position—is used in campaigns, elections may make a difference in policy. To the extent that the second method of presentation—creating positive images of oneself and negative images of one's opponent—is used, campaigns will tend only to reinforce existing opinions, and will have few observable consequences for policy.

Foreign aid and related questions were discussed by the two Presidential candidates in 1960 almost entirely by appealing to the known or assumed preferences of those the candidates were addressing. There was, for example, much mention of the Food for Peace program—but always before farm audiences concerned about agricultural surpluses. Praise of various countries and national heroes was frequent in speeches to nationality-group audiences. (On one occasion Nixon felt obliged to offer a somewhat apologetic explanation for talking about Nigeria—in addition to Italy, of course—before the Columbian Republican League.)[21]

But the most significant technique of the candidates was the use of foreign affairs to exemplify the two major competing issues of the campaign: Nixon's "experience" vs. Kennedy's "movement and innovation."

Kennedy formulated his appeal at one of his first formal campaign appearances:

I do not feel that the last years have been so successful that we should move from those to an endorsement of a previous action. I don't think you can suggest to me

37

one new program in the field of foreign policy which had had general acceptance around the world that has been developed in the last year[s]. Nothing comparable to the Marshall Plan, to NATO, to Point 4. I think what we need is a new administration with new people, new vitality, and new ideas.[22]

Nixon similarly used arguments from foreign policy to emphasize his basic themes. The following exchange is from a news conference in the first month of the campaign:

Question Do you mean to imply . . . that Mr. Kennedy is espousing a surrender policy toward the Soviet Union [in suggesting that President Eisenhower should have expressed regret over the U-2 flight]?

The Vice President Absolutely no. Mr. Kennedy didn't know what he was espousing. That was the trouble. I've indicated time and again that Mr. Kennedy is a man that is just as strong against communism as I am, and as most Americans are, but I indicated that in this view [of his], because of perhaps lack of understanding and experience he was naive. . . .[23]

These themes were repeated in the basic speeches of the two candidates throughout the campaign.[24]

The specific foreign policy issues on which the candidates disagreed are a further indication that foreign affairs did not afford meaningful policy choices to the electorate. For the most part debate was more tortuous and sophistic than enlightening on Khrushchev at the United Nations, policy toward Cuba, and the problem of the off-shore Chinese islands, Quemoy and Matsu.[25]

The treatment of foreign affairs by Nixon and Kennedy often illustrated more about the candidates than about the issues. Kennedy demonstrated the practicing politician's conception of foreign affairs. He constantly linked domestic policies with foreign policy, as when he connected the accomplishments of the welfare state with opportunities overseas: "Franklin Roosevelt was a good neighbor around the world because he was a good neighbor in the United States."[26] Or, in a more general linking of domestic and foreign activities:

> During the American Revolution, Thomas Paine wrote, "The cause of America is the cause of all mankind." I think in 1960 and in the next decade, the cause of all mankind is the cause of America.[27]

Foreign aid and, indeed, all of America's international endeavors were discussed by Kennedy in terms of a pervasive instrumental approach and a strong concern for international opinion, both of which characterized the cooperative activism of his administration. The success or failure of the United States' competition with Russia was judged according to whether Soviet or American leaders and deeds were most prominently displayed in the foreign press; the Republican treatment of Asia and Africa stood condemned because no current American statesmen were being quoted in those regions, and because the governments of those areas were no friendlier to America than they had been eight years previously.[28]

Nixon's approach, on the other hand, included a much broader philosophical appeal. He occasionally took advantage of one of the more naive cultural lags by holding out the possibility of effective foreign aid on the cheap, as opposed to "others" who wanted merely to spend wildly in the underdeveloped countries.[29] But basically he appealed to a transcendental belief in the divinity of the American past and the innate charity of the American present to justify current international activity:

> Look at the history of America. One hundred and eighty-five years ago we were a very weak country militarily compared with the other world powers. We were a very weak country economically and agricul-

turally, and very little industry to speak of, but we were one of the strongest nations in the world and the peoples in the world. Why? Because we stood for ideals that were greater than America. Ideals that belonged to all humanity. Ideals that came not from men but from God, and I speak of faith in God, faith and respect for the dignity of all men, regardless of their background or their race or color. Recognition of the fact that freedom and independence—these words which sometimes we take for granted because we have enjoyed them so long—that they belong not only to us, but that they belong to peoples throughout the world on both sides of the Iron Curtain.[30]

This philosophy leads directly to a support for foreign aid:

When we talk about what we're going to do in this field of foreign assistance, we're helping the Nigerians, and we're helping the Indians, and the other people, remember, we do this not solely for the negative reason that we're trying to keep what we've got, that we're trying to keep communism from spreading in the world. We do it because we Americans traditionally have had a heart.[31]

The one partial exception to this pattern of indirect argument occurred late in the campaign. On November 2, Kennedy proposed establishing:

a peace corps of talented young men and women, willing and able to serve their country . . . for 3 years as an alternative or as a supplement to peacetime selective service.[32]

Kennedy thus proposed a real alternative for consideration, taking, incidentally, the first step toward what came to be one of the more important and popular innovations of his administration.

Nixon's reply shows how one candidate can prevent serious consideration of meaningful alternatives by refusing to debate an issue. On November 6, Nixon issued a statement condemning the plan as "superficial and obviously concocted for campaign purposes." He proceeded from irrelevancy to hyperbole in attacking the idea of a peace corps without actually discussing the plan as it had been put forth by his opponent.

> It would [said Nixon] be harmful both to the Selective Service and to those so ably representing the U.S. abroad. . . . It would set up an "elite" corps who would be excused from military duties. This would be a class distinction completely alien to our heritage. . . . Mr. Kennedy would cater to draft evasion. He would develop a "cult of escapism."[33]

So much for the only concrete new departure in foreign policy suggested by either candidate in the course of the campaign.

The foregoing demonstrates that, in 1960 at least, foreign policy in general and certainly foreign aid policy, were dealt with in such a way as to hinder rather than promote meaningful electoral choices. In the words of John Hightower, the 1960 campaign was most significant for what was not said. The commitment to American participation and leadership in international affairs was shown by the fact that neither candidate made any sort of isolationist appeals.[34]

The electoral audience which the two candidates apparently had in mind closely parallels the kind of audience which has been described by academic studies of voters and voting.[35] Essentially this is an audience with a continuing interest in foreign policy and a general presumption in favor of external contacts by the United States. But it is also an audience in which the amount of attention and level of information are so low, and the interrelation of opinion so complex, as to raise major barriers to the creation of significant foreign policy electoral issues. A chief exception is when a candidate takes a foreign policy stand so extreme that his opponent can exploit his position by appealing to a "common sense" approach. This is what happened to Goldwater in 1964 on the issue of "nuclear responsibility."[36]

This description of the electorate is supported by studies going back to the 1948 Presidential campaign. When the results of poll questions on foreign aid are tabulated according to party, there are no significant or consistent differences. In addition, while adherents of the Democratic and Republican Parties do take opposing stands on some foreign policy questions around election time, the evidence suggests that they adopt what they believe to be the position of their party, rather than identifying with a party because of its stand on foreign policy issues.[37] Voters are more likely to divide sharply on "questions which personalize party conflict than . . . on questions of a more ideological character. . . ."[38] They also occasionally perceive party or candidate differences on foreign policy greater than the facts would warrant. In the 1948 Presidential campaign both Harry Truman, the Democratic incumbent, and Thomas E. Dewey, the Republican candidate, advertised with about equal fervor their toughness toward the Soviet Union. Yet in one local study of the election 30 per cent of the Republicans responding to an interview asserted that their candidate, Dewey, favored taking a firmer stand with Russia than did Truman; and a like number of Democrats judged Truman to be tougher than Dewey toward the Soviet Union.[39]

Regarding even basic knowledge of partisan positions on issues, Angus Campbell and his colleagues have found that concerning foreign aid only about one respondent in five had, at the same time, an opinion, any knowledge of government policy in the field, and an accurate perception of policy positions of the two parties.[40]

But these findings do not fully account for the campaign treatment of foreign aid. There are many issues whose complexities surpass the analytical abilities and inclinations of the rank-and-file voter, such as agricultural policy, government intervention in the economy, the proper extent of social welfare measures, even broad foreign policy issues such as the degree of firmness with which Russia should be faced. Yet on many of these issues one finds that voter information and interest is higher, and campaign arguments much more sharply stated, than on foreign aid. Even the alleged "me-too" campaign of Richard Nixon made clear his differences with Kennedy over such questions as policies toward the farmer, government health insurance, aid to education, and government spending in general.

One reason for greater precision in these areas is the widely observed tendency for higher levels of information and interest to be associated with "bread and butter issues." But this is not the full story. The issue on which the greatest number of respondents (more than one-third) showed knowledge and perception of party positions was in the field of foreign affairs—the question of taking a firm stand against China and the Soviet Union.[41]

There is an important reason why foreign aid receives especially ambiguous treatment in the partisan political process. Foreign aid offers no opportunity for candidates to tap a consistent set of opinions. As pointed out in Chapter 2, the opinions and attitudes necessary for support of foreign aid are internationalism, including long-term involvements with foreign nations, a belief in the exportability of the "American way of life," a tolerance of "deviant" international behavior on the part of aid recipients, and a certain amount of sanguineness about governmental spending.

We have already seen how these beliefs may work against one another in some cases. Support for aid on the basis of exporting "Americanism" will tend to decrease tolerance for neutralist and socialist foreign governments. Acceptance in principle of unpopular and unfamiliar behavior patterns may often be accompanied by a decreased willingness to become extensively involved with other nations.

Furthermore, these values are diffused throughout American society, not concentrated in a politically effective fashion. Foreign aid thus falls into a pattern consistent with what we know about the interplay of values relative to foreign affairs. Internationalism (whether the expansionist or cooperative version) and isolationism, on the one hand, and various domestic beliefs on the other, have existed historically in a series of changing associations which defy analysis or generalization.[42]

The past is rich in examples. Consider the following statement of a Republican official serving a Democratic President, concerning his administration of aid to war-torn Europe:

> My job was to nurture the frail plants of democracy in Europe against . . . anarchy or communism. And communism was the pit into which all governments were in danger of falling when frantic peoples were driven by the Horsemen of Famine and Pestilence.

While the words could very well be those of Paul Hoffman, the first administrator of the Marshall Plan, the speaker in this case was Herbert Hoover, Woodrow Wilson's Relief Administrator at the end of World War I. The last stage of Hoover's career saw him cast in the role of defender of the faith of economic conservatism behind the wall of a fortress America. But in earlier years he was an active prophet of Wilsonian internationalism, casting out the devils of deprivation and preaching salvation through a belief in democracy and sound business principles.[43] Both positions have been, and still are, representative of large elements of American thinking. Hoover's early reputation was sufficiently persistent to induce President Truman to ask him to serve again as a "Relief Ambassador" after World War II.[44]

Present-day American society contains intricate combinations of pro- and anti-aid attitudes. Individuals at the upper scale of income and status are among the most internationally inclined. They travel the most, read the most public-affairs magazines and newspapers, and discuss international issues. This helps create a favorable attitude toward foreign aid. On the other hand, these groups are also the most conservative economically. Their antipathy to government spending counteracts, at least in part, enthusiasm for foreign aid.

Lower socioeconomic groups operate from a reverse set of motivations. Their feelings run strongly toward the nationalist, hard-line style of foreign policy. The risks involved in aid to underdeveloped, neutralist nations seem scarcely worth the effort. They are, however, much less concerned about government spending. Government programs, domestically at least, benefit them more than other groups.[45]

Comparing two of the attitudes favorable to foreign aid, internationalism and economic liberalism, Key has shown that high levels of both occur together in only about 9 per cent of the population. The conjunction of internationalism and conservatism occurs in 5 per cent, isolationism and liberalism are espoused by 14 per cent, and the most anti-aid combination, isolationism and conservatism, occurs in 12 per cent of the sampled population. (Excluded from these figures are those who wish to keep the economic status quo and those with no opinion.)[46]

Patterns of conflicting opinions can also be uncovered by comparing the poll eliciting opinion on the Peace Corps, which offered a good index of opinions on cooperative internationalism, with the results of a question on government spending and the level of taxation, which provided an indicator of domestic conservatism.[47] By dividing the population according to occupation and cross-tabulating the rankings on the two questions we get results somewhat different from Key's, but still showing the majority of the population (55 per cent) in the two ambiguous positions, internationalist-conservative and isolationist-liberal. The remainder is divided equally between the strong pro- and anti-foreign-aid combinations.

We can further assess the political implications of opinion by examining the taxes vs. spending question. As we said, when respondents who favored reduced spending were asked to name those policies they considered most eligible for government economies, they frequently mentioned foreign aid. However, those same respondents are *more* favorable than the other groups to the kind of foreign aid represented by the Peace Corps. The high levels of Peace Corps support come about largely because this particular program is strongly supported by some groups which have low levels of approval of foreign aid in general.[48] A reason for this was suggested by former Peace Corps Director Sargent Shriver:

> We appeal to the spirit of personal initiative, to the spirit of volunteering to do something for your country, to be patriotic. These are some of the qualities that right wing people look for in the American personality and character.[49]

Pressure Groups and Foreign Aid

A more nearly complete picture of the role of pressure groups must await later consideration of how they deal with the legislature and the executive. We can show at this point, however, the fragile base from which they operate, as well as some of the barriers they encounter in trying to influence policy.

Estimates of the actual or potential extent of group activity concerning foreign aid vary tremendously depending on the criteria used. In terms of groups who might intervene because of economic interests, there are over 5,000 firms which have had foreign aid contracts with the government since 1954.[50] Around twenty groups can be expected to turn up at any congressional hearing on foreign aid legislation. A *Congressional Quarterly* report on "Opposing Lobby Groups Active For, Against Foreign Aid," listed only six groups as being actively concerned with this area of policy.[51] But there are ten or twelve groups which do some or all of the following: make a continuing study of foreign aid, regularly send out publicity on the subject, make contact with the executive branch, and discuss foreign aid with legislators. This does not take into account those individuals, groups, and business firms which from time to time exhibit specific concern with foreign aid, since their intermittent actions generally do not affect the general outlines of policy.[52]

Associated with the small number of actively concerned groups is their relative lack of power in the decision-making process—a phenomenon attested to by those on both the sending and receiving ends of pressure-group activities. We can highlight the barriers these groups encounter if we consider some conditions for influencing policy, such as: the group should have a spokesman able to speak confidently on behalf of a large group of clients (proportional to the number affected by a policy) strongly favoring a given set of policy ends and means; the issues involved should be of sufficiently narrow scope so that party considerations are not important; the nature of the issues should be sufficiently "technical" so as not to involve major ideological complications; the spokesman should have a clear, concrete, and legitimate interest in the policy the group is proposing; and the spokesman should have as much, if not more, knowledge of a subject as the public official before whom representations are made. The more frequently these conditions prevail, the more important will pressure groups tend to be. When, as in the case of foreign aid, these conditions are not present, groups tend to observe rather than influence the policy-making process.

The first negative factor is the nature of the groups' constituents and the policy preferences they hold. We have already seen that there are no easily identifiable segments of the population which feel strongly either for or against foreign aid.[53] Furthermore, public arguments concerning foreign aid contain elements which are unrelated and inconsistent. Not only do opposing sides often talk past one another—a common feature of political debate—but even those nominally on the same side frequently contradict one another.

One favorable group will argue on behalf of foreign aid because it is an expression of the disinterested humanitarian concern that Americans have for the less fortunate of the world. Another will invoke the allegedly powerful anti-Communist and friend-winning powers of foreign aid. Still another will assert the long-run benefits of aid which disinterestedly promotes the growth and independence of foreign nations. Nodding in the direction of a balanced presentation, advocates frequently interlace their internationalist presentations with heavy doses of reformist demands, calling for better coordination, elimination of waste and corruption, and improved personnel policies, an approach characterized by Senator Stuart Symington as "sort of like being for early spring and against sin. . . ."[54]

At the other extreme are the opponents of the program, who also present a variety of conflicting arguments. Foreign aid, they contend, is bad because it has not worked: aided countries are still in economic difficulties. Foreign aid is also bad because it has worked too well: industries in aided countries are becoming dangerous competitors to American businesses. Others point out that foreign aid is wrong because it is not mentioned in the Constitution. Still others use the public administration argument to say that aid should be done away with because it has not been administered efficiently. Extreme opponents have more exotic arguments: foreign aid is a Communist idea, part of the plan to get America to spend itself into bankruptcy. (One cannot help wondering whether Soviet Russian premiers, in planning their country's foreign aid program, must prevail over colleagues who are sure that the idea of foreign aid is part of a capitalist plot to dissipate the resources of revolutionary Russia.)

A third group, which overlaps the first two, consists of those who wish to promote specific goals by giving foreign aid. These groups rely on their economic or philosophical interests to form the analogies by which they judge policy. They include those stirred by a combination of international generosity and a high regard for particular aspects of American life; business groups that desire to transmit the blessings of free enterprise abroad; labor unions that view with suspicion any aid programs not directly concerned with strengthening foreign labor movements; the champions of cooperative movements; and Americans favoring the use of foreign aid to obtain a more democratic Spain, Portugal, Yugoslavia, or Poland.[55] In this same "coattail" category are groups desiring policies to promote specific economic interests. Much congressional hearing time is taken up by those who wish to see that no assistance is given to certain kinds of industries abroad, to urge that certain commodities be used in the aid program, or to see that aid be withheld from governments until they pay various claims, damages, or debts alleged to be due to American citizens.[56]

Such fragmented and disjointed arguments by pressure groups tend to intensify, rather than alter, the prevailing lack of agreement as to what should be discussed in the debate over foreign aid. They offer little help to the principal audience of their discussions, the congressmen, who must usually react to foreign aid as a whole.[57] Furthermore, each specialized appeal in the absence of consensus becomes a further step away from a meaningful debate over policy. In fields where a consensus does exist, special interest appeals may lead to marginal modifications of policy. But a collection of narrow arguments, in the absence of consensus, merely adds to the pressure for a fragmented, uncoordinated consideration of policy.

A second obstacle to significant pressure-group activity is the fact that the issues involved in foreign aid are of sufficiently broad concern to be taken up by many participants in the political system. Whatever may be said about the inability of the major parties and their spokesmen to offer meaningful alternatives in the area of foreign aid, both parties are concerned with foreign aid, and do attempt to establish partisan positions regarding it.

The fact that foreign aid encompasses so many conflicting attitudes requires pressure groups to spend much of their time addressing the public and their own members in order to explain and to argue the correctness of their position. They are consequently unable to center attention on directly supporting or modifying government policy. Many staff members of pressure groups, when interviewed, mentioned the need for frequent communications of their group's position on foreign aid to their membership and the public. The Committee for International Economic Growth (CIEG), which favored the aid program, reported sending an average of about 300,000 pieces of information a year to the public. This material consists of between 100 and 200 separate books, articles, pamphlets, and newspapers. The anti-aid Citizens Foreign Aid Committee (CFAC) mails a weekly newsletter to about 4,000 subscribers.

The mere fact of communicating with the public does not necessarily indicate weakness; it is an activity in which nearly all groups engage. In fact, the CIEG and CFAC staff each optimistically looked upon its large mailings as a positive sign of great public interest in and enthusiasm for its point of view.[58] A pro-aid labor official, on the other hand, acknowledged the need for periodic communication with the membership in order to maintain, or even create, the rank-and-file opinions on foreign aid which the Washington office wanted to represent. This latter situation, described by several pressure-group representatives, adds a new dimension to the weakness of groups which promote general and intangible interests.[59] While some groups consume resources in communicating with those who already agree with them, others are forced to expend energy and money to convince their own membership.

The problem of information and knowledge remains the final factor inhibiting effective pressure-group action. Some idea of the vastness and complexity of the subject with which these groups deal can be gained from the fact that foreign aid projects cover as wide a range of activities as those handled by the federal government within the United States. Indeed, with the increased attention paid to long-range economic planning the government is now participating abroad in projects from which it is proscribed at home. Not only is there a mass of technical detail involved, but there are different requirements for application in each of the nearly 100 countries which have received assistance.

Most groups are severely disadvantaged when it comes to mobilizing knowledge and expertise for analysis of the foreign aid program. In contrast to the hundreds who collect information in the executive branch, and the scores who evaluate this information in the legislature, only one pressure group investigated in this study had more than one or two employees (and many had none) working full time on foreign aid. In most instances groups are so lacking in knowledge that they can merely rephrase old arguments for or against the program.

The one group which does have more than minimum staffing on foreign aid is the National Chamber of Commerce. The Chamber has three full-time staff members who study and analyze the foreign-aid program submitted by the executive branch. Their commentary, in the form of draft testimony, is checked by other staff members of the Chamber who are specialists on agriculture, labor, and commerce. (The Chamber has a staff with competence in almost every category of the federal budget and annually prepares its own "anti-budget" in reaction to executive branch proposals.)

The testimony is then approved by a special subcommittee of the Foreign Policy Committee, the full committee, and the Board of Directors of the Chamber. After approval is given, the witness—usually a business-man with international experience—is brought in for a dry run on the testimony, a process which includes going over with the witness questions it is felt the congress-men may ask.

Such detailed procedure allows the Chamber, which generally supports foreign aid, to propose more detailed spending cuts and to offer criticism in greater scope than any other nongovernmental group. The figures recommended, as one staff member said with some pride, are consistently quite close to the amount finally ap-propriated.

However, even a group as thorough as the Chamber cannot realistically expect to be treated with the same solicitude as well-informed groups in other areas of policy. In fact, a group may harm its arguments by knowing too much as well as by knowing too little. This was the unusual situation in which the witness for the Chamber, Mr. Forest Murden, found himself when ap-pearing before the Senate Foreign Relations Committee in 1961. In his testimony, Mr. Murden had spoken of the fact that only "a handful of Congressional staff" was available to study foreign aid. This led to the following exchange with Senator Stuart Symington:

Senator Symington Now, I am interested in the ques-tion of how recommended reductions were arrived at, how you arrive at these reductions.

You mentioned yourself there are many thousands of employees in the AID, but that there is only a "handful of congressional staff."

You have not too much of a staff that can handle this $4.7 billion to $3.6 billion in the Chamber, have you?

Mr. Murden No, we have a small staff, Senator, that works with this program over the year.

Senator Symington How many people?

Mr. Murden   Dr. Nystrom here has a staff of three people.

Senator Symington   Three?

Mr. Murden   Yes.

Senator Symington   I would think what would be sauce for the goose would be sauce for the gander, too.[60]

In addition to the problem of analyzing technical information there is a more general problem shared by all pressure groups: the acquisition of political intelligence. What are the various public audiences of significance and what kinds of appeals should be made to them? Some groups apparently lack even the most fundamental knowledge in this field. In a discussion of public opinion and foreign aid, one anti-aid group representative showed himself unaware of the extensive public polling which has been done when he said:

That's a very important and difficult field. I really don't know what public opinion is on foreign aid. *If* Gallup would take a poll on it, since he's in favor of foreign aid, he would probably find the majority of people in favor of aid too. [Italics added.]

We can end this chapter by restating the point made at the beginning. The values affecting opinion on foreign aid are interrelated in a wide variety of ways; opinions themselves are widely diffused throughout American society. Partisan electoral activities and pressure groups —the standard political links between the governed and the government—fail, in the case of foreign aid, to have great influence on policy-making. Foreign aid involves the American population directly and indirectly—in selling to the government, in working for it, in concern with government spending, and in other controversial ways. Many groups pay some attention to foreign aid. Yet both the making of policy and the relevant discussion and debate on policy still come almost exclusively from the formal decision-makers in Congress and the executive. Congress, as the ratifier of values and principal policy-maker, will be our next concern.

4

Congress and Foreign Aid

The public at large may think, feel, or exhibit "moods"; party spokesmen and electoral candidates may argue and advocate; lobbyists may testify and try to persuade; but Congress—unlike any group studied so far—has an integral part in determining policy. Consequently the opinions and attitudes of Senators and members of the House of Representatives take on special significance.

In American politics the national legislature is the target for suggestions, requests, and appeals from all manner of constituents, special interest groups, party leaders, and administrative officials. Not only is the congressman an individual who observes the world from the perspective of a particular background and set of beliefs—congressmen of course use simplifying analogies as do the rest of us—but he is also a participant in the governmental system, expected to reconcile a host of parochial demands on his time, energy, and view of the world in order to help make national policy. Thus a legislator is not simply a fifty-year-old lawyer from a Midwestern small town. He is also a Republican member of the Committee on Agriculture concerned about the growing power of the Secretary of Agriculture. His votes on foreign aid may be shaped by unconscious reference to the economy of his home state and by puritanical values of thrift and self-reliance. But they may also be shaped by the way in which he perceives opinion in his district and by whether or not a President of his party is occupying the White House. A congressional staff member once put it concisely: "A Congressman is just like anybody else except he knows how to get 50,000 people to vote for him."

Outlines of Congressional Response

We can begin to see the complexity of the factors bearing on foreign aid voting by comparing congressmen with the total population in terms of background characteristics associated with favorable or unfavorable opinions on foreign aid.

First, many congressmen come from backgrounds associated with favorable opinions on foreign aid. Only those persons engaged in professional, managerial, and sales occupations scored an average of 60 per cent or more in favor of foreign aid. While these groups constitute only 29 per cent of the national adult population, they make up well over half the membership of both houses of Congress.[1] Proportionately more congressmen than the public at large have also received some college education, another factor associated with support for foreign aid.

On the other hand, the point has already been made that in both the House and the Senate there is overrepresentation from those geographical regions least favorable to foreign aid. The high proportion of representatives of rural districts in the House, at the expense of suburban and urban districts, creates a further unfavorable situation. Residents of agricultural areas have indicated to pollsters the greatest opposition to foreign aid.[2]

In two recent Congresses, Senators and House members averaged favorable roll-call votes on foreign aid and related policies about 60 per cent of the time, a figure somewhat above, but close to, the approval levels in public opinion surveys.[3] Such figures cannot, of course, be treated as the equivalent of opinion survey results. Among other things we are here studying behavior—votes—in order to infer opinions, reversing the procedures often used in polling. Furthermore, institutional factors of procedure and structure must always be taken into account in analyzing legislative voting. For example, the average support figures for the Senate and House are 52 per cent and 63 per cent respectively. This difference does not mean that the House is more favorable than the Senate toward foreign aid, but may be attributed largely to the fact that the House, unlike the Senate, considers legislation in such a way that many restricting amendments and cuts in funds are not decided by roll-call votes.

Analysts of congressional behavior typically view legislators from five different perspectives: the congressman as the target of pressures from his party, from pressure groups, and from his constituents; the congressman as a participant in internal congressional politics; and the congressman as both partner and competitor with the executive branch. The present chapter will discuss congressional decision-making on foreign aid policy in terms of the roles of pressure groups, public opinion, party and intra-congressional forces. The fifth category, congressional-executive relations, will be discussed in the next chapter.

Pressure Groups and Congress

It has been pointed out that pressure groups appear to play only a small role in the formation of foreign aid policy. Occasionally, they have been able to form alliances with interested congressmen to modify a foreign aid bill to their liking. Some recent trends in aid policy

are undoubtedly beneficial to domestic American interests. Examples include the increasing tendency to pur-
chase aid commodities in the United States, restrictions
on aid to nations which expropriate American property,
and aid funds earmarked for subsidies to home-building
abroad. Many groups, such as the National Association
of Home Builders, see such changes in policy as a victory
for them, but the arguments in favor of the changes are
usually broad in scope. Government officials, whether
sincerely or expediently, discuss these policies in terms
of their general benefits.[4]

Certain groups, such as labor unions, have easy
access to many members of Congress. The spokesmen of
these groups are able, therefore, to communicate their
feelings on foreign aid in an effective fashion. However,
domestic issues are both the reason for the access and
the prime concern of the representatives of these groups.
Only minimal attention is paid to foreign aid.

Most pressure-group influence on foreign aid is so
small that it would scarcely be considered at all in other
areas of public policy. One pressure-group spokesman
admitted that not many congressmen attended the hearings at which he testified. But he recounted with evident
satisfaction that he had been assured by a member of
the committee staff that even though many committee
members might be unavoidably absent, they all had
assistants present who were listening carefully.

Another knowledgeable respondent was quick to
assert that groups favorable to foreign aid could be
effective. He cited as an example the League of Women
Voters, which had sent a telegram of complaint to Representative Otto Passman (D., Louisiana), Chairman of
the subcommittee which handles foreign aid appropriations. Although possibly successful as nuisance-value,
the telegram and the congressman's response can scarcely be considered an example of pressure-group victory.
Congressman Passman's reply called the League "pre-
sumptuous" for placing its own "limited knowledge"
ahead of his and that of his supporters.[5]

Although the public record may supply only meager evidence as to the role of pressure groups, such statements as do appear correspond to the picture drawn from private interviews. Proponents of aid rarely mention specific nongovernmental groups, either ignoring the question of noncongressional sentiment, or claiming support for foreign aid on the part of the public at large. Congressional opponents likewise ignore those groups which echo their position, and dismiss pro-aid groups as naive "do-gooders," or selfish profit-seekers.[6] Indeed, when Congressman Passman himself later turned to outside groups such as the "Liberty Lobby" for support in his effort to reduce foreign aid appropriations, this was considered a sign of the decreasing power of anti-aid legislative forces.[7]

The Role of Party Affiliation

By contrast, the factor of party appears to have a good deal of bearing on congressional voting. Although the Presidential candidates and formal platforms of both major parties have endorsed foreign aid,[8] the political history of aid and the general orientations of Democrats and Republicans toward it provide the basis for discernible party differences.

First of all, Democrats have been more closely associated than Republicans with the development of the program. Two of the most famous texts in the history of foreign aid—the "Marshall Plan" speech at Harvard University in 1947, and President Harry Truman's Point Four program of technical assistance to underdeveloped countries—are associated with Democratic administrations. Although sometimes cooperative in supporting aid programs, especially the Marshall Plan, Republicans nevertheless have shown themselves more critical of foreign aid, and more willing to restrict its operations and reduce its size.

Later in this chapter we shall see how Congress,

like the public, reacts to foreign aid in terms of general images. Many of these images are shared by members of both parties, but certain beliefs which lead to antagonistic reactions to foreign aid probably occur more widely among Republicans than Democrats. Especially important in provoking negative feelings are increased activity and spending by the federal government, and deep involvement with policies of foreign nations.

The figures on foreign aid voting by party in the 86th and 87th Congresses show a tendency toward greater support for foreign aid by Democrats than by Republicans. In the House of Representatives the average Democrat voted supporting foreign aid 68 per cent of the time. The corresponding figure for Republicans was 54 per cent. In the Senate the average figures for Democrats and Republicans were 53 and 48 per cent respectively. From the point of view of distribution of congressmen, 82 per cent of House Democrats have average scores of 50 per cent or better; only 60 per cent of Republicans scored above 50 per cent. In the Senate 70 per cent of Democrats and 60 per cent of Republicans scored 50 per cent or better on foreign aid voting.

If the scores for voting on foreign aid are plotted to show the percentage of congressmen in each decile of support, from 0 to 100, the members of the House from both parties fall into a reasonable approximation of a "J-curve," indicating a strong tendency toward consensus, with the Democrats having slightly more scores at the high levels of support and fewer scores at the lower levels. In the Senate the scores demonstrate a bimodal distribution, with the Democrats again having a slightly greater number of high scores, proportionately, than Republicans[9] (see Figures IV-1 and IV-2).

The workings of party factors become effective through the electoral and other political processes. For a congressman, one of the chief elements of the political process is his relationship to the President. The average votes for foreign aid, it will be recalled, were derived from the period 1959-1962, comprising two years each

Figure IV-1. VOTING SUPPORT FOR FOREIGN AID IN THE HOUSE OF REPRESENTATIVES, 86th AND 87th CONGRESSES

% of each party

Support for aid (deciles)

Democrats _____ (87th Congress)
Republicans _ _ _ _ _ _ _ (86th Congress)

of Republican and Democratic incumbency in the White House. Sharp differences emerge when voting on foreign aid for these two periods is compared.

Most members of the House and Senate shifted their positions rather substantially between the two Congresses. Cross-tabulating foreign aid support scores (by deciles) for the 86th and 87th Congresses provides the following results: in the Senate only 17 per cent of the senators (15 out of 86) appeared in the same decile of support in both periods. For the House this figure is 28 per cent (99 out of 357). Furthermore, those with no shift in position were principally those who either consistently supported or consistently opposed foreign aid. In the Senate those who supported aid less than 20 per cent of the time, and those who supported aid at least 80 per cent of the time, supplied fourteen of the fifteen senators who had no shift in position. In the House nearly nine-tenths of those without a shift in position were consistent supporters and opposers.

If we include those who shifted no more than one decile in either direction, the numbers are still relatively small. This category includes 19 per cent of the Senate and 23 per cent of the House. This means that for about two-thirds of the Senate and half of the House of Representatives, a member shifted his position by 11 percentage points, at the very least, between the period 1959-1960 and the period 1961-1962. Members whose support for aid was in the 50 per cent decile in one Congress, for example, scored at least 60 per cent or less than 40 per cent in the other Congress.

The direction of these changes can be seen from the percentage of congressmen found in each decile of support for foreign aid. As might be expected, the shifts are clearly in the direction of support for the President of a legislator's own party. These patterns can be seen most clearly if we observe how each party voted with its own President in comparison to how it voted with the President of the opposition party. Thus we compare the votes of Republicans in the 86th Congress with the votes

Figure IV-2. VOTING SUPPORT FOR FOREIGN AID IN
THE SENATE, 86th AND 87th CONGRESSES

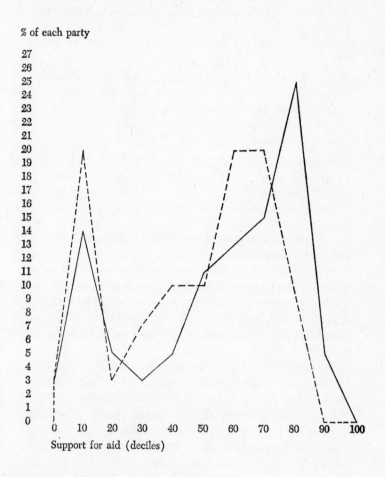

% of each party

Support for aid (deciles)

Democrats _____(87th Congress)
Republicans _ _ _ _ _ _ _(86th Congress)

of Democrats in the 87th Congress for patterns of Presidential support; we make the reverse comparison for patterns of Presidential opposition (Figures IV-3 to IV-6). The percentages by party can be compared in Table IV-1.

Table IV-1. AVERAGE SUPPORT FOR FOREIGN AID BY PARTY (IN PER CENT)

House of Representatives	Demo-crats	Repub-licans	Over-all Average
86th Congress	64	62	64
87th Congress	78	53	69
Both Congresses	72	58	67
Senate			
86th Congress	52	67	57
87th Congress	65	40	56
Both Congresses	59	54	57

These comparisons show several things; both Democrats and Republicans exhibit strong patterns of consensus when voting with the President of their own party. When voting on the foreign aid proposals of the opposition party's President, both senators and representatives fall into the kinds of bimodal distributions associated by public-opinion analysts with patterns of conflict.

Furthermore, both parties contain small contingents of "die-hard" supporters and opponents of aid who remain at one end or the other of the scale irrespective of the party affiliation of the President. This is especially evident in the House of Representatives where there is a group of Democrats (about one-fifth of the Democratic members) which voted 100 per cent in favor of foreign aid during both the Eisenhower and Kennedy years. Conversely, there is a group of about the same proportion of Republicans who fell in the deciles of 20 per cent or below even during the two years of Eisenhower. The corresponding groups of Kennedy-supporting Republicans and Kennedy-opposing Democrats also existed, but in smaller numbers.

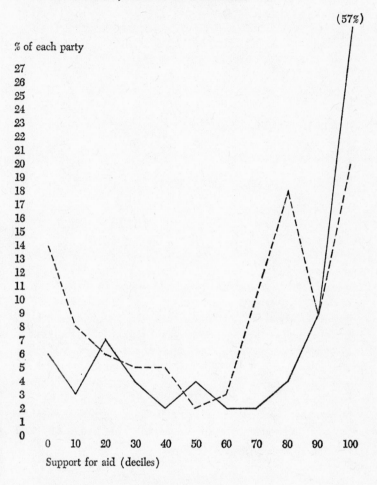

Figure IV-3. FOREIGN AID VOTING IN SUPPORT OF PARTY'S OWN PRESIDENT, HOUSE OF REPRESENTATIVES

(57%)

% of each party

Support for aid (deciles)

Democrats _____ (87th Congress)
Republicans _ _ _ _ _ _ _ (86th Congress)

Figure IV-4. FOREIGN AID VOTING IN SUPPORT OF
PARTY'S OWN PRESIDENT, SENATE

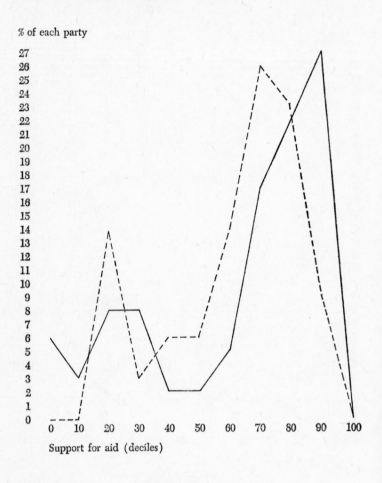

% of each party

Support for aid (deciles)

Democrats _____ (87th Congress)
Republicans _ _ _ _ _ _ _ (86th Congress)

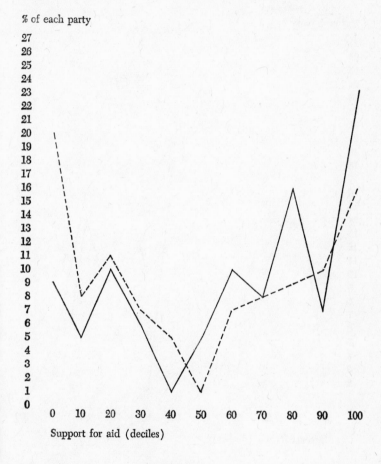

Figure IV-5. FOREIGN AID VOTING IN SUPPORT OF
OPPOSING PARTY'S PRESIDENT, HOUSE OF REPRESENTA-
TIVES

% of each party

Support for aid (deciles)

Democrats _____ (87th Congress)
Republicans _ _ _ _ _ _ _ _ (86th Congress)

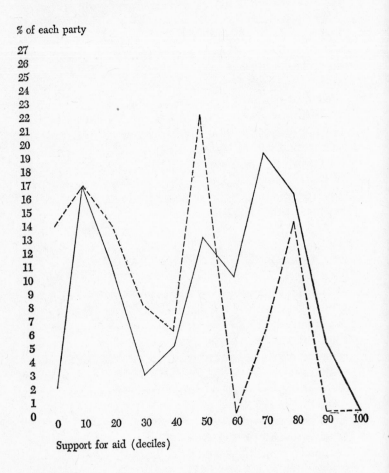

Figure IV-6. FOREIGN AID VOTING IN SUPPORT OF
OPPOSING PARTY'S PRESIDENT, SENATE

% of each party

Support for aid (deciles)

Democrats _____(87th Congress)
Republicans _ _ _ _ _ _ _(86th Congress)

The period under study has frequently been characterized as one of "bipartisan cooperation in foreign aid"; in reality it has been something quite different. There was control of the legislature by a party which had a majority supporting its own President on foreign aid as well as a minority faction which supported even an opposition President on foreign aid. Both Eisenhower and Kennedy received support for aid principally from their own partisans in Congress.

The role of the President and his officials in mobilizing support for the program offered by the executive branch will be discussed in succeeding chapters. At this point we can note that while the party affiliation of the President is highly significant in determining the patterns of support and opposition to foreign aid, there are many other influencing factors.

Internal Congressional Influences

Within this framework of support and opposition Congress makes many decisions about the composition of the aid program. These decisions are of such detail and complexity as to be beyond the knowledge and understanding of most constituents; they are so numerous and comprehensive as to be beyond the attention of most lobby groups; and they are frequently made in such speed and disorganized fashion that the executive branch has little chance to advocate its own preferences.

For much of the decision-making on foreign aid the legislator is unable, even if he so desires, to react to specific inputs of information, requests, or pressures. He must draw upon the "capital" of pre-existing attitudes affecting behavior. Many of the factors influencing decisions on aid are found in the structure and procedures of the two houses of Congress.

It is well known that the American national legislature contains many individuals and groups with more power than others. Likewise, the rules and procedures give some courses of action advantages over others. This situation has been seen by different observers as the deliberate arrogation of power by a few congressmen, as an anachronistic "obstacle course" working against rational law-making, or as merely the need for organization within a complex institution. Whatever combination of causes one selects, the conditions must be taken into account in any study of law-making.

The disposition of foreign aid by the legislative machinery might well be summarized in Professor Richard Neustadt's phrase, "emergencies in policy with politics as usual."[10] The procedures which have evolved for the treatment of foreign aid demonstrate anomalous characteristics. On the one hand, foreign aid is often debated in terms of the most extreme policy alternatives. The advocates invoke the full gamut of historical mission, cold-war dangers, and impelling national interest in support of the program. Opponents allege massive waste and corruption, general ineffectiveness, and threats to the integrity of the dollar.

The rhetoric associated with debate over aid calls to mind some of the great congressional struggles over foreign policy in recent American history—neutrality legislation of the 1930s, Lend-Lease, the Marshall Plan, the North Atlantic Treaty Organization, and the extensions of Presidential tariff-cutting power. In these cases congressional leaders, along with others outside Congress, played important roles in employing their powers of persuasion, bargaining, and barter in the endeavor to help the President's programs overcome powerful opposition. The publicity and uncertainty attending these decisions not only made strong leadership necessary but also provided the opportunity for the tools of leadership to be used effectively.

The treatment of foreign aid today, however, no longer takes on the dimensions of "emergencies in policy." Instead, the standard patterns by which Congress deals with foreign aid can be characterized as "politics as usual." This means, to paraphrase Woodrow Wilson, that congressional decision is essentially committee decision.

As the congressional treatment of foreign aid has assumed an annually recurring pattern, attitudes of members have become fixed.[11] In these circumstances the personal appeal or the particular legislative barter loses its effectiveness. This repetition also means that, as with most legislation, the committee reporting a bill will in general be upheld by the full membership. Members normally support a committee decision because they tend to be informed about only two kinds of issues—those which are unique and dramatic, and those within the jurisdiction of the members' own committees.

There is also a strong tendency for members to support bills originating in their own committee. In the Senate (where frequent roll calls lead to more diverse voting records) 50 per cent of the members of the Foreign Relations Committee supported foreign aid at least 70 per cent of the time. In the rank-and-file of the Senate only 39 per cent were found in the 70 per cent decile or higher.

In the House of Representatives this same pattern prevails. At the level of 70 per cent or more support for foreign aid were found 80 per cent of the House Foreign Affairs Committee. (Twenty-one of thirty committee members voted for aid legislation at least 90 per cent of the time.) Among rank-and-file members 62 per cent were found at the 70 per cent decile or above.

Both the House and Senate Appropriations Committees, on the other hand, exhibit less voting conformity. In the Senate Committee, only 32 per cent of the members supported aid by at least 70 per cent. In both the full House Appropriations Committee and the subcommittee on Foreign Operations (where most of the decisions on appropriations are made), there has been an approximate 50–50 division between those above and those below the 70 per cent level of support. The division in the subcommittee is particularly sharp. There were no members at all in the 50–70 per cent range. Six of the members voted for aid programs 80 per cent of the time or more; the other five supported aid 40 per cent of the time or less. As we shall see, the two appropriations committees are fully as able as the authorizing committees to have their reports approved, despite their lack of voting solidarity.[12] See Table IV-2 for the relative support given by committee members.

Table IV-2. AVERAGE SUPPORT FOR FOREIGN AID BY COMMITTEE, 86TH AND 87TH CONGRESSES (IN PER CENT)

	House of Representatives	Senate
Foreign Affairs or Foreign Relations Committee	83	65
Appropriations Committee	57	53
Foreign Operations Appropriations Subcommittee	59	—
Other Committees	67	56

The relative success of the committees in having their reports approved is at the heart of "committee government" in Congress. This success can most clearly be shown by examining the levels of funds approved at various stages of the legislative process. Table IV-3 summarizes this information for the six fiscal years 1958-1963, showing the average percentage change occurring at each stage of congressional consideration.

The maximum average change on the floor of either house was 5 per cent, the amount by which the Senate reduced the figures of its Foreign Relations Committee. In every other instance a committee's recommendations were not changed by more than 2 per cent. The number of times a committee's fund recommendations were approved without change illustrates the same point. In the six-year period studied, the number of times there were no changes is as follows: Senate Foreign Relations Committee, three; House Foreign Affairs Committee, four; Senate Appropriations Committee, six; House Appropriations Committee, four.

Table IV-3. AVERAGE CHANGES IN FOREIGN-AID FUNDS MADE BY VARIOUS UNITS IN THE LEGISLATIVE PROCESS, FISCAL YEARS 1958-1963 (IN PER CENT)

Authorization (Over-all average reduction, 8 per cent)

Senate Foreign Relations Committee	-2^a
Senate	-5^b
House Foreign Affairs Committee	-8^a
House	-1^b
House-Senate Conference	-1^c

Appropriation (Over-all average reduction below authorization, 10 per cent)

Senate Appropriations Committee	-5^d
Senate	0^b
House Appropriations Committee	-18^d
House	$+2^b$
House-Senate Conference	-5^c

[a] Executive branch requests used as base.
[b] Relevant committee report used as base.
[c] Maximum passed by either house used as base.
[d] Authorization limits used as base.

This power stems in part from the advantages shared by all congressional committees; the specialization of knowledge about a complicated policy question; the inability of noncommittee members to become fully acquainted with the issues; and the tradition that a committee which has heard testimony as an agent for the whole Congress and which has carefully studied the legislative matter possesses authority which merits deference.

These values were well expressed in 1960 by Representative George Mahon (D., Texas), then the second-ranking member of the House Appropriations Committee. He opposed an amendment increasing the foreign aid appropriations although he personally favored a higher figure. It would be wrong, he said, to repudiate the work of the subcommittee which had put long hours of careful study and hard work into its report.[13]

THE POLITICS of AMERICAN FOREIGN AID

Power, like beauty, is partly in the eye of the be-holder. In most situations, the would-be exerciser of power must be able to judge the reactions of those over whom power is to be exercised. For committees as well as individuals, power is relative rather than absolute. Consequently, legislative decision-making takes on the characteristics of an extensive guessing game. Both the authorizing and appropriating committees must try to anticipate the "mood" of their own houses in terms of the acceptable levels of funds and qualitative restrictions surrounding the program. In the incident noted above, Congressman Mahon went on to illustrate this "guessing game" approach. In arguing against the House's raising appropriation figures he said that if higher figures were really needed, the executive could make appeals to the Senate Appropriations Committee.[14]

For three of the relevant committees "the law of anticipated reactions" has required estimating how much they can recommend without provoking major cuts by the House or Senate. With the Subcommittee on Foreign Operations of the House Appropriations Committee the problem has been to gauge how *little* can be reported without incurring a "revolt" which would increase the funds. Since the recommendations of the Appropriations subcommittee must be approved by the full committee, there also exist the possibilities for an intra-committee guessing game. During the tenure of Clarence Cannon (D., Missouri) as Appropriations Committee Chairman, there was close cooperation between him and Subcom-mittee Chairman Passman. There was never any doubt that the full committee would approve the subcommit-tee's large cuts in aid funds which amounted to about 20 per cent of the sum already authorized. Chairman Cannon had, in fact, placed Congressman Passman at the head of the subcommittee because of his known willingness to reduce the aid program. In 1964, when Cannon died and Representative Mahon became chair-man, things became more complex. Mahon was unwill-ing to support the same degree of fund-reduction which had pleased his predecessor. He therefore exercised his formal and informal powers as chairman, including the right to vote as a member of the subcommittee, to oppose Passman. In cooperation with party leaders in the House and officials in the Johnson Administration, Mahon was able to effect a "turnaround" in the subcommittee and hold cuts to a minimum. Once this was achieved, the patterns of deference to subcommittee and committee action worked to assure an aid bill that contained funds much closer to what had previously been authorized.[15]

In addition to judging what their own house will support, a bill's floor leaders must keep in mind what the other committees and the other house have already done or are likely to do. In 1962 both the House and Senate cut foreign aid expenditure requests by 4 per cent. These cuts were made in different segments of the bill, however. In the conference to resolve House and Senate differences each side accepted the larger figures of the other, and the final authorization was only 2 per cent below the Administration's figures. In the same way, administrative restrictions considered undesirable may be accepted in one house if it is anticipated that they can easily be eliminated in conference.

This game may occasionally have the opposite result. In at least one recent instance the Senate failed to play its expected role and made sharper monetary cuts than the House, with the result of unexpectedly low appropriations.[16]

The Senate Appropriations Committee, the final committee reporting on foreign aid each year, plays a particularly important part in these maneuvers. Since its members are at least moderately favorable to foreign aid, and since it usually does not act until the House has dealt with appropriations, it has come to be regarded (with no little resistance among committee members) as a "court of last resort" for the aid program.[17]

The process of "anticipatory bargaining" is complicated by the fact that every participant is aware of what the others are doing. There is, consequently, an attempt by each side to push its own position to the fullest in order to obtain the best possible bargaining position. Restraints on participants exist largely in the possibility of being overridden on the floor.

For all the importance of committees, the total membership still retains its role as a "gun behind the door" which may, and sometimes does, significantly alter committee decisions. We have seen that there are occasional revisions of the amount of money recommended by the committees. Later we shall consider qualitative amendments introduced on the floor. Most important, much of what the committees do is in anticipation of what the membership will accept. The ranges of tolerance, while wide, do have limits.[18]

Public Opinion and Congressional Opinion

What determines the limits of acceptability? We have already seen that party attitudes account for much of the voting on foreign aid. But there appears to be another factor at work as well—general opinion on foreign aid.

One indication of the relationship between opinion and congressional behavior can be found in Table IV-4. The table presents a comparison by geographical regions of public opinion responses and the levels of congressional voting support for foreign aid. There are relatively close correlations between public opinion in most geographical areas and the attitudes of their representatives. Only in the Rocky Mountains is there a great divergence. These figures and the average congressional voting scores, mentioned above, indicate the possibility of some connections between constituent opinion and voting.[19]

There are two likely explanations for the coincidence of public opinion and congressional behavior. Either the public has strong wishes which it communicates to congressmen in an influential manner, or both the congressmen and the public act on the basis of common perceptions and beliefs. While evidence shows both explanations to have some validity, the latter case—legislative action on the basis of widely shared values—is the more influential regarding aid.

Turning first to the possibility of direct public influence, we note that most Congressmen, when referring to public opinion in their formal statements, try to give the impression of merely ratifying the overwhelming sentiment of their constituents in voting for or against foreign aid.

The opponents of aid are especially prone to invoke the "will of the people" in advocating their position.[20] The evidence supplied by legislators, in fact, clearly lends itself to the inference that the public, as it impinges upon Congress, is strongly opposed to aid. Many more opponents than supporters cite the wishes of the people in defending their positions. Personal interviews in Congress confirm this impression of a public which is perceived from Capitol Hill as hostile to foreign aid.

Table IV-4. SUPPORT FOR FOREIGN AID IN PUBLIC OPINION POLLS AND CONGRESSIONAL VOTING, COMPARED BY GEOGRAPHICAL REGIONS*

Region	Opinion Poll	Senate Votes	House Votes
Rocky Mountains	1	5	6
New England	2	1	1–2 (tie)
Mid-Atlantic	3	4	1–2 (tie)
Pacific	4	3	3
East Central	5–6 (tie)	2	5
West Central	5–6 (tie)	6	4
South	7	7	7

* Rank numbers indicate descending order of support

As for letter writing, the situation appears to be clearly the opposite of the tendency, suggested by Key, for the public to write letters of approval rather than disapproval.[21] In interviews with congressmen and staff, both those strongly favoring aid and those opposing it, it was reported that mail almost always ran heavily against foreign aid. Supporters insist that the letter writing is largely the result of organized campaigns on the part of relatively small, intense segments of the public. Opponents, not surprisingly, see the mail as a more accurate indicator of public sentiment.

The nature of constituents' letters and other such uncertain indicators of opinion as direct-mail surveys are only part of the difficulty of assessing the influence of opinion. The political significance of public opinion derives not from what a certain segment of the population believes at a given moment, not even if that segment believes strongly enough to write letters. It derives from how voters in general will react during a political campaign, especially when a congressman's position on a particular issue is used by his opponents.[22]

For some congressmen there is an identity between the opposition to aid expressed by mail and the political potency of opinion: "If I were running for membership in the House against an incumbent who voted for this [foreign aid] bill," said one Southerner, "I would base my campaign on that one vote—and would win, hands down. The tone of my mail from my own constituents is such that I would be ashamed [afraid?] to face them if I should vote to extend the program." He went on to say that he was sure this same situation prevailed across the nation, in every congressional district.[23]

In contrast is this statement of President John F. Kennedy: "Contrary to repeated warnings, in the seventeen years since the Marshall Plan began, I have never heard of a single politician who lost his office by supporting foreign aid."[24]

The truth of the matter is probably that congressmen do not know the political significance of the distribution of opinion on foreign aid. There are few professional polls on the subject conducted even at the state level; before 1963 there were apparently even fewer conducted in congressional districts.[25]

The barriers to direct constituency influence are increased by the general low importance given to questions of foreign aid by voters.[26] Under these conditions a legislator may be forced to become a Burkean in spite of himself. This does not mean that he makes judgments in a political vacuum. We have seen that he may turn to the colleagues of his party for guidance, or follow the wishes of the President. He may also rely on his own generalized images of the world, reacting on the same basis as those he represents and thereby developing views that parallel the opinions of his constituents, even when he is uncertain as to what those opinions are.

In previous chapters we discussed the "pictures in our heads" which help form opinion on foreign aid. One reason for supposing that congressmen are influenced in the same way has been suggested by Lewis Anthony Dexter. The importance of the decisions which congressmen make does not necessarily change them as individuals or change their means of making decisions. Dexter notes:

> we tend to conceive [of] Congressmen [as] tackling highly responsible choices with the same care and awe with which we tackle or feel we ought to tackle the few responsible choices we make. But in the nature of their very lives, Congressmen can't do this—nor . . . can they work out the pros and cons on each issue with the care applied by a scholar writing about what they did.[27]

Just as obscurity and the lack of personal impact force "the man in the street" to resort to a general *Weltanschauung* in thinking about foreign policy, the frequency and rapidity of decisions about these same questions force the congressman to rely, at least in part, on general images and perceptions of the world. This may be true even for those congressmen whose legislative positions allow them to have direct contact with foreigners and to observe the results of foreign aid in person. As one congressional staff member put it:

> It's very hard to say what influence the Committee's trips abroad have. One thing is that there is not much tangible evidence of all the money we have spent in these areas. People tell us that a certain mill or factory is more productive than before, but it is very hard to specify what the actual results are.

This feeling plus the numerous conflicting reports by congressmen after inspection trips of the same areas of the world recall the well-known psychological phenomenon that pre-existing assumptions and expectations are as much a part of the "real" world as direct evidence of the senses.

In Chapter 2 public attitudes were examined in terms of three standards by which foreign aid is judged: traditional responses to international relations including both the desire to spread Americanism and the fear of becoming overly involved; the needs of cold-war diplomatic strategy; and general attitudes about governmental economic policy. It was seen how each of these standards could be used for either support or opposition to various aspects of foreign aid. These same three standards also appear to be of major importance in congressional decision-making. For congressmen there is an additional criterion which might be termed the constitutional standard—the proper division of power between Congress and the Executive.

Legislative procedures, unlike the polling techniques, do not normally present individuals with relatively simple and abstract questions on whether they prefer aiding allies or non-allies, or whether they desire programs with low or high overseas involvement. A legislator's choices will generally be much more complex: will a member support increasing funds for military aid, involving more government spending, aid to allies and the risk of high involvement—thereby upholding the desires of the President, but at the same time rejecting the recommendations of a congressional committee which has carefully studied this question?

A few aspects of foreign aid are so clearly defined in terms of general attitudes that congressional reaction to them can be viewed as reaction to a distinct set of values. Response to the Peace Corps is such a phenomenon. Advertised as a means of stimulating American patriotism and transmitting it abroad by means of modestly-paid, noncareer volunteers, the Peace Corps has been accepted on these terms by Congress and firmly endorsed.

Particularly instructive was congressional treatment of the Peace Corps in 1962, the second year of legislative consideration. The funds voted were nearly double the appropriation in 1961. The amount—$59 million—was 93 per cent of the original request. In the House the appropriation bill was carried 317–70, receiving the support of better than eight of every ten voting members. In the Senate both the authorization and appropriation processes were approved with voice votes.

In both 1961 and 1962 the congressional debate was highly laudatory—in part to the Peace Corps, in part to its director, Sargent Shriver, and in part to the America which was sending its citizens abroad "to mingle with the common people," as one Southern congressman said.[28] "To know America is to love America," said another member by way of explaining his enthusiasm for the Peace Corps.[29] The program was also seen as a welcome alternative to diplomacy conducted by professionals: "Most of our diplomats do not have that personal touch with the man in the street in the countries to which they are assigned."[30]

Even objectors to the program did not question the people-to-people missionary ideal. They simply regretted its being tarnished through association with the government. Said one member:

I believe that it [the Peace Corps] represents a mistaken effort to secularize and socialize the type of

81

humanitarian activity abroad long and successfully promoted by missionary movements and nongovernmental philanthropies.[31]

Others who voted against the program praised the soundness of its missionary principles, but objected to a doubling of the agency's spending in its second full year of operation.[32]

The general patterns of congressional thought can also be indicated in part by the amendments offered to foreign aid bills during floor debate. The kinds of changes various members desire in the program is a reflection of what they think the program is and what they feel it should become. In the period 1959–1962 there were 137 amendments offered in the Senate and 163 in the House of Representatives.[33] Of these, approximately 30 per cent (41 in the Senate and 46 in the House) were of a miscellaneous variety.[34] The classification of the remaining 70 per cent is reported in Table IV-5.

This table shows the House and Senate differing in two respects. The Senate is more willing than the House to alter the military component of the aid program, and it is also more willing to use the program as a means of assisting the private sectors of the economy. Otherwise, the two houses exhibit similar patterns of behavior. Amendments designed to control the activities of aided nations show a relatively high rate of approval. This appears to be a manifestation of the desire to deal with a world which is as much like America as possible. When the world does not adhere to this pattern, an attempt is made to make it conform. It would be something of an understatement to point out that this is a difficult endeavor. The chairman of the Senate Foreign Affairs Committee, J. William Fulbright (D., Arkansas), expressed his displeasure at such attempts during a debate on an amendment to control the interest rates at which foreign aid money would be lent within recipient countries. Addressing himself to the sponsor of the proposal,

Table IV-5. FLOOR AMENDMENTS OFFERED TO FOREIGN-AID
LEGISLATION, 86TH AND 87TH CONGRESSES

TYPE OF AMENDMENT	% of All Classifiable Amendments		% of Each Type Approved	
	SENATE	HOUSE	SENATE	HOUSE
Economic Aid (procedures and levels of funds)	23	24	36	43
Military Aid (procedures and levels of funds)	17	14	44	25
Increase Congessional Control	23	26	59	68
Assistance to U.S. Economy	15	17	53	35
Influence or Control of the Behavior and Policies of Other Nations	22	19	67	68
Totals	100	100		
(N)	(96)	(118)		

he said, "If the Senator knows how we could legislate on this floor to change the interest rate in Chile or Brazil I think he would be a genius. I do not think we can do so."[35]

The intractability and the vagaries of international events can frustrate those who praise foreign aid by pointing to showcases abroad as well as those who try to insist upon foreign rectitude as the price of foreign aid. Recent events in Southeast Asia give the following colloquy a sharp ironical twist. The exchange occurred in 1959 during Senate tributes to Ngo Dinh Diem on the occasion of his fifth anniversary as leader of South Vietnam:

Mr. Keating Mr. President, we hear a great deal about the attacks on our mutual security programs, and about the areas where it has not done as much as was anticipated. Is not South Vietnam an outstanding example of the credit side of the ledger, so far as our mutual security program is concerned?

Mr. Sparkman   I think the question answers itself. It certainly is.[36]

This desire for certainty in areas where change and uncertainty are widespread provides much ammunition for opponents of the program. Congressman Walter Judd (R., Minnesota), in urging support of the program, once pointed out that all the arguments about government spending and "fiscal responsibility" could also be used against the defense budget, which was ten times the size of foreign aid. A rebuttal came from one congressman who said he had voted for defense and would vote against foreign aid "because I have a greater faith that the political philosophy of this country will be stable as it is, for the next two years, than in some of the other countries."[37]

This part of the American tradition of foreign relations permits two alternatives—either to deal with other nations so as to have as little involvement with them as possible, or to try to influence other nations into patterns which conform to American experience and expectations. World events since World War II have made the former approach almost impossible, and so the latter has been adopted. But the desire for noninvolvement is not completely dead. Consider this proposed amendment to foreign-aid legislation:

> It is the sense of the Congress of the United States that the great rule of conduct for us, in regard to foreign nations, is in extending our commercial relations to have with them as little political connection as possible. So far as we have already formed engagements let them be fulfilled with perfect good faith. Here let us stop.[38]

In urging its adoption the proponent of the amendment reminded his colleagues that the text was taken directly from George Washington's Farewell Address. It was nevertheless defeated. It was sponsored by Congressman H. R. Gross (R., Iowa), well-known in the House as a constant opponent of all manner of government spending. The episode cannot be dismissed, however, without noting that Congressman Gross has since been appointed to the House Foreign Affairs Committee, of which he is now a member.

Applying economic criteria to foreign aid has resulted in mixed reactions to the program. On the one hand, proponents use the argument that aid funds, up to 80 per cent of which have been spent in the United States, stimulate the economy and provide more jobs for Americans. There are two arguments against this position. The first, a technical one, holds that the effects of aid are minimized because the goods purchased are sent out of the country, and are unavailable for domestic consumers. The second argument, more sweeping and more widespread, attacks the program from the point of view of fiscal orthodoxy. It considers any government spending to be dangerous, especially in connection with an unbalanced budget and balance of payments problems. Those programs for which there is an uncertain rationale, such as foreign aid, thereby come under strong fire from this point of view. Dahl has cited instances of these arguments in the earliest considerations of the Marshall Plan.[39]

More than fifteen years later these negative arguments are still prevalent and apparently quite influential. Senator Everett Dirksen (R., Illinois) has expressed this position with characteristic flourish. He also added another example of viewing foreign societies in terms of assumptions about one's own. "The recipients of the largess under this bill," he said, "are in their condition in large part, at least, because of their fiscal difficulties." It is therefore America's duty to avoid this same fate: "if the country which administers these benevolences, if we wish to call them that, should founder on the same rocks, what would any foreign-aid program mean? Our first line [of defense] is the fiscal integrity of this country."[40]

The final chief object of congressional concern is the effect of foreign aid on the manner in which power is shared by the legislative and executive branches of government. The wide discretion given the executive branch has been lauded in some congressional documents. In the words of one report:

> The Congress has wisely provided to the Executive flexibility by refraining from establishing country ceilings in the appropriations (thus permitting shifts in country allotments within an appropriation), by authorizing a contingency fund, and by permitting limited transfer between appropriations.[41]

More typically, congressmen have given vent to their frustrations at such grants of authority. There is a strong consensus in Congress—among liberals as well as conservatives—that the legislature must maintain a constant alert to see that it does not lose out in its never-ending constitutional tug-of-war with the executive branch.[42] This fear was voiced by Congressman Porter Hardy (D., Virginia), former chairman of the subcommittee which oversees administration of the foreign-aid program. He proclaimed that "annual review of the program is little more than an empty ritual" because of the secrecy and high-handedness of the executive branch.[43] (Also see the high rate of approval of amendments designed to increase congressional control, Table IV-5.)

The most common charge against the executive branch is the alleged incompetence and even dishonesty of those who administer the program. Always careful to distinguish between the President himself and alleged "little bands of willful men" in the State Department, the aid agency, or in the aid missions abroad, critics invoke images of widespread waste of public funds to justify the need for closer congressional control.[44]

The other side of the coin of bureaucratic inadequacy is congressional legitimacy and wisdom. Close congressional scrutiny is one means for aid supporters to justify themselves to unhappy voters. One congressman indicated that in answering letters from constituents who complained about foreign aid he always made it clear that "we should keep the program under constant examination and re-examination, because we all realize that the program involves immense sums of money. . . ."[45]

Finally, close congressional control is also held by some to be a necessary ingredient for an acceptable aid program. The following extract from debate in the House of Representatives, while somewhat more lyrical than most, is an example of frequently-expressed views:

The fact is that our diplomats and foreign aid administrators are less qualified to make . . . judgments [on economic development policy] than the Congress. Most of them are career State Department people with little or no experience in the workaday world they seek to establish for recipient nations. On the other hand, look about you in this great legislative hall. All about you are doctors, lawyers, labor union leaders, carpenters, teachers, farmers, scientists, ministers, mothers, fathers, children, and grandchildren. Whatever is America you will find here in this House. This is cross section U.S.A.: New York, Chicago, "Punkin Center," Tex., San Francisco, Florida, Utah, and all points in between. This is America.[46]

We can conclude by noting that Congress may be part of America, but is not all of it. It may be that part of America which feels the need to extend its power abroad but is not sure how to do it; it may be that part which recognizes the need for government activity, even while fearing the government's increase in power and spending; it may be that part divided by images of what the world is like and preferences as to what the world should be like; and it may be that part united to some extent by party affiliations and regional attitudes. But if it is the America which has met payrolls and carried precincts, it is not the America which has observed the economic and political problems of underdevelopment, formulated plans to counter these problems, and attempted to win approval for the plans. It is to this latter task, the role of the executive branch in seeking support for foreign aid, that we shall now turn.

5

The Executive As Organizer

of Attitudes

The primary initiator and organizer of opinions about foreign aid is the executive branch of government. The history of foreign aid is principally the history of policy initiatives taken by the President and his advisers—postwar relief, the Marshall Plan, assisting underdeveloped countries, the emphasis on military programs after the Korean War, and a revived interest in economic development in the late 1950s and early 1960s.

The sources of executive branch power in foreign policy-making are the same as those which have led to the growth of executive power in other areas of national policy: the need for problem-solving and decision-making based on a high degree of specialized knowledge, extensive resources for collecting, evaluating and storing information, and over-all coordination of this knowledge. As the technical need for the management of information has increased, so has the size and activity of the federal bureaucracy. The need to make quick policy decisions has meant a growth of activity and discretion in the upper levels of the executive. As Richard Neustadt has pointed out, even Dwight Eisenhower, with his relatively passive conception of the Presidency, carried out the kinds of policies and took the kinds of decisions which in earlier days would have classified him as an exceedingly strong and active chief executive.[1]

Such changes have been even more marked in foreign than in domestic policy; and in the realm of foreign policy they have been especially important in respect to foreign aid. The planning and execution of a successful aid program requires information about the political, social, and economic situations in the nearly one hundred nations which receive aid. This has presented American diplomats with increasing demands. In addition, foreign aid draws upon a range of knowledge and skills at least as broad as that needed in all the rest of the government. From public health to public works, from the successful exploitation of agricultural resources to advice on the creation and maintenance of a commercial airline, the variety of projects which constitute the aid program represent a near-microcosm of the activities of the private and public sectors of American society.

It is also important for the executive branch to instigate action in foreign aid. Many elements of the opinions and attitudes among the public and Congress have provided at best a mixed, and in some respects a negative, impulse to government activity in the field of foreign economic development. If there is to be a foreign aid program at all, the executive branch must work actively for its acceptance and continued support.

It is generally assumed that the practitioners of foreign policy perceive and respond to problems in their domain quite differently from the public and Congress. Having more frequent and intimate contact with international events, and deriving their livelihood from managing these events successfully, foreign policy officials frequently develop styles of thought and reach conclusions which are rarely shared, let alone understood, by nonprofessionals. The fact that there is a foreign aid program at all in the face of hesitancies and doubts of the public is a major evidence of some differences. Yet it is important to note how much of the official description, explanation, and justification of foreign aid is consistent with the values which have already been found among the public and legislators.

Philosophical Justifications for Foreign Aid

As we look at the manner in which foreign aid has been defined and defended by officials of the executive branch, we are confronted with many familiar themes: the revolutionary, missionary spirit, touched with humanitarian concerns; expectations about the conformity of other nations with American standards of international behavior; and the desire for a relatively low-cost, unentangling aid program. The Truman, Eisenhower, Kennedy, and Johnson Administrations have differed in the emphasis given to these themes, but they all expressed them to some extent.

President Truman's 1949 Inaugural Address, which launched aid for economic development, contained many familiar concepts. The extension of American values abroad: "What we envisage is a program of development based on the concepts of democratic fair-dealing." Humanitarianism: "Only by helping the least fortunate of its members to help themselves can the human family achieve the decent, satisfying life that is the right of all people." The desire for an inexpensive program: "The material resources which we can afford to use for the assistance of other peoples are limited. But our imponderable resources in technical knowledge are constantly growing and are inexhaustible." Simplistic American reverse-Marxist assumptions about economics and international relations: "Greater production is the key to prosperity and peace"; and the genesis of applying standards of international behavior to aid recipients: assistance

91

was to be given only to "peace-loving" and "free" peoples of the world.

In the years following, justification for the program has proceeded on two levels. The first is the strategic or instrumental approach. Aid is presented as a means of permitting continued access to areas important to American interests. This has been applied chiefly to military aid, but it also relates to economic development. Unless America participates in the defense and development process, so the argument goes, the United States may not have ample opportunity for its counsel to be heard in international dealings. The United States also stands the risk of being excluded from important raw materials, and from opportunities for profitable trade and private investment. This "hard-headed" approach foresees aid as a worthwhile expenditure from a strict calculation of national advantages. When Douglas Dillon was Under Secretary of State during the Eisenhower Administration he put the matter quite clearly: "I am an investment banker by trade, and I speak as an investment banker when I say that today's less developed nations are tomorrow's richest economic and political asset."[2] President Kennedy spoke of how foreign aid gives American businessmen access to otherwise closed markets, often inducing foreign consumers to develop preferences for American products.[3]

A slightly different expression of the same approach has been used in the "no Communists with full bellies" argument. Arising from the notion that increased wealth prevents totalitarianism, it has posited aid as "the use of material means to a non-material end"—free, or at least non-Communist, political systems.[4]

This instrumental approach, particularly its strong anti-Communist aspect, has been attacked by liberals and conservatives alike as being inadequate, inaccurate, or both. Many commentators have pointed out the dangers which arise from justifications for aid in terms of material self-interest or hard-line anti-Communism. The truth is that neither of these instrumental arguments has been widely used by the executive branch. There has been instead more frequent use of the broad philosophical themes enunciated in President Truman's Point Four speech designed to reconcile American conceptions of international politics with the acceptance of a foreign aid program.

The first attempt at reconciliation has been to define foreign aid as "exporting the American idea, the American Revolution, or the American dream."[5] The messianic connotations implicit in President Truman's description of "technical missionaries" at work in foreign aid are an example.[6] In 1953 a State Department spokesman answered the rhetorical question, "How shall a Christian look at Point Four?" with the Biblical injunction: "Verily I say unto you, in as much as ye have done it unto one of the least of my brethren, ye have done it unto me."[7]

For Secretary of State John Foster Dulles the historical tradition of America included Christian impulses favorable to foreign aid:

Our forebears [he said] believed in a Divine Creator who had endowed all men with certain inalienable rights. They believed in a moral law and in its concepts of justice, love, and righteousness. They had a sense of mission in the world, believing it their duty to help men everywhere to be and to do what God designed.[8]

The secular background of America was also considered a foundation for defending foreign economic aid. The high international ideals and moral force of the United States, held to be powerful even when American politics were isolationist,[9] were seen as being furthered in foreign aid programs.[10] In discussing this missionary, value-exporting aspect of foreign aid, Secretary of State Dean Acheson on one occasion appeared as an early prophet of the Peace Corps:

I have often wondered whether that spirit of adventure and hardship still exists in the United States. I think it does, but I think it is an open question. I wonder how many volunteers from all our colleges, who are graduating this June, you would get if you went to them and said, "I want to offer you a hard life; you are not going to be paid much; you are going to live in backward areas of the world where there is disease lurking everywhere; you are going to work and to live with people who know nothing and are going to be very suspicious of you. . . . Will you go out and take this missionary task with you?" I think we would be surprised. I think a lot of boys and girls would do that.[11]

Republican officials stressed the same theme, if in a somewhat more passive and automatic variation:

the political revolution which created the United States has had a greater influence for good on the rest of the non-Communist world than any other single political event in history. That influence is still visibly strong and vital. Since World War II, nations comprising a billion people have found inspiration in our example in establishing the framework of their new, free societies. They now look to us for assistance in realizing the material fruits of freedom.[12]

With the establishment of the Peace Corps by the Kennedy Administration, this ideal was transformed into reality. Secretary of State Dean Rusk expressed his feeling that "the most important of all the benefits of the Peace Corps" would not be the substantive contribution to economic development, but rather "an unprecedented opportunity for the nations and peoples of the world to learn what America is all about, what it stands for, what it and its people are really like."[13]

In emphasizing the traditions of America which were being furthered by the foreign aid program, there have been frequent references to business, as well as ideological, missionaries. High on the list of exportable items have been the virtues of private capitalism and free enterprise. The earliest descriptions of the Point Four program emphasized that small amounts of technical assistance were expected to serve as seed-beds for increased trade and private investment, which would then be the chief source of capital for economic development.

Part of the reason for emphasizing the role of private enterprise has undoubtedly been the desire to obtain the most assistance for economic development for the least expenditure of tax dollars. If the relatively inexpensive technical assistance program had, in fact, led to private trade and investment, the Truman, Eisenhower, Kennedy, and Johnson Administrations would have been able to conduct their foreign policies with much less domestic turmoil.

The appeal of the market as a means to economic development also stems from the American desire to remain, as much as possible, aloof from political connections with aided countries. Using models derived from nineteenth-century international financial practices (and ignoring the calamities of the pre-World War II period), these arguments pictured the need to reconcile international economic policies with the laws of the marketplace as the road to development requiring the least political interference.[14]

Underlying the arguments in favor of private channels of support for economic development there appears the assumption, often implicit, that this is the "natural" course of international economic relations. Supporting this approach, government spokesmen have invoked images of ancient traders who extended technical progress with their investments. Presuming natural harmonies to result from private trade, official spokesmen have metaphorically extended the beneficent "invisible hand" of private investment as a means of assistance to the underdeveloped areas of the world.[15]

It is questionable whether the kinds of policies outlined above were appropriate to the "real world" of the underdeveloped nations. Many writers have strongly suggested that they were not. It has been noted that trade between diversified industrialized economies and primitive economies dependent on a single crop or commodity may increase rather than decrease the gap between the two. The export earnings of underdeveloped economies may not enter the sectors of the economy most crucial for industrialization. The general fear and hostility felt toward private investment by many leaders in underdeveloped nations are also cited as additional barriers to private capital investment.[16]

But it is not necessary to use technical analysis to discover problems in the reliance on private trade and investment. The statements and policies of the executive branch point these out quite clearly. The most obvious example is the contradictory manner in which the executive branch presented its case to the public. While many officials, as noted above, were using nineteenth-century examples and analogies to describe policy goals, others —not so highly placed—were describing the contemporary irrelevance of the nineteenth-century economic system.[17]

Policy-makers have encountered serious resistance in trying to develop trade and investment as politically neutral means of achieving development. It has frequently been necessary for executive officials to give very political lectures to American businessmen on their "inertia" and "insularity." They have also approached the limits of diplomatic protocol by complaining that the domestic philosophies and policies of the underdeveloped countries are insufficiently receptive to the blessings of private investment.[18]

The goal of free market development has been hampered by the unwillingness of the recipients to believe the official description of business investment as nonpolitical and therefore desirable. In extolling the virtues of international private investment one spokesman cited American business in Canada where, he said, the people would "deeply resent" any suggestion that investments have an undesirable impact on their political life.[19] This was just four years before the American Ambassador to Canada was forced to take note publicly of rather strong suggestions by Canadians that such undesirable impact was in fact occurring.[20] Similarly, the prologue to one of Vice President Richard Nixon's "six crises"—his encounter with angry Latin American mobs —may have been mentioned by a State Department official in 1956. He described the "encouraging spectacle" of Latin America as the underdeveloped area with the "soundest," "most stable," and "mature" relations with the United States, since its dollar income consisted of the highest proportion of private, nongovernmental funds.[21]

As events failed to bear out the expectations of policy-makers, the policies regarding capital investment have had to be altered.[22] We might note here a minor irony in the timing of this change of policy. Events permitted the Democrats to maintain high hopes of private investment for economic development through 1952 when they relinquished control of the executive branch to the Republicans. The Democrats were able to justify such government capital as was furnished as merely the "necessary equipment" accompanying technical assistance, and as emergency stop-gap measures until private investors would begin to do their work.[23] Republicans could be expected to be even more eager than the Democrats to "unleash" private enterprise for development purposes. Yet by the end of their term of office in 1960 they found it necessary to establish a new government agency, the Development Loan Fund, to provide the capital which was not forthcoming from the business community.

There are two points of particular interest in this change of policy. It was adopted only after an apparent search for any possible alternative to direct governmental loans. And it has been accompanied by arguments and descriptions which attempt to link the new policies as closely as possible with the old assumptions. Both the search for alternatives and the traditionalist arguments have been used by Democrats as well as Republicans.

One alternative, discussed since Point Four days, is

the offer of guarantees and inducements to businesses which invest in underdeveloped countries. The other alternative—perhaps more accurately described as a hope —has been to expect existing institutions to fill the need for development capital. Essentially this meant looking to the Export-Import Bank.[24] This institution showed the double advantage of being both fiscally sound—that is, a profit-making enterprise—and philosophically straight —working through private businesses.

Although the EXIM Bank has operated throughout the period of foreign aid, it became clear by the late 1950s that it would be insufficient to do the job expected of it. Despite references to the EXIM Bank as the source of development capital for Latin America, Africa, and other areas,[25] it could be so considered only on the basis of the rather ingenuous assumptions outlined above about trade and private investment as the key to foreign economic development. For the Bank, which was originally established in the 1930s as an anti-Depression device, is essentially a means of promoting American exports through short-term, dollar-repayable loans to foreign customers of American businesses. In official discussions of general economic policy, the EXIM Bank has frequently been characterized as a device for promoting trade rather than as a source of development assistance.[26]

In the closing years of the Eisenhower Administration these weaknesses of the Bank were officially acknowledged.[27] The Development Loan Fund was consequently established to provide the long-term, low-interest loans which came to be seen as necessary to promote economic development.

The creation of the DLF did not, however, mean abandoning the official position of hopeful expectation that private investment would eventually play the major role in providing capital for developing nations. If anything, the explanations of DLF policy laid even greater stress than before on the traditional theme of the importance of private investment.[28] These arguments emphasized that DLF operations were of a temporary character and would be characterized by a lively concern to avoid competition with private investment. It was promised that the DLF would "consciously and energetically assist and promote the activities of private industry and enterprise."[29] Vance Brand, the first Director of the DLF, attempted to defend the propriety of the philosophy of his agency:

> When I say *American private enterprise,* I mean every one of the three words. *American* enterprise, simply because the record proves as a fact that American industry has unexcelled resourcefulness, initiative, and creativity. . . . *Private* enterprise, because I believe the peculiar problems of economic development require the talents of men who have proven themselves as producers and enterprisers. . . . And *enterprise*—that word is perhaps the key to the whole concept, because, without the spirit of drive and initiative which it implies, development simply cannot take place. . . . So when you put all three words together—*American private enterprise*—you have what to my mind is unquestionably the most powerful and effective force . . . that can be applied to any problem or task of economic development.[30]

He went on to reassure any doubters that his celebration of the business spirit was "not due to any narrow or chauvinistic or doctrinaire reasons."

> DLF's job [he said] is to stimulate economic development; I want it to do its job; I want it to use the best means available in doing so; and American private enterprise is the best means. That is all there is to it.[31]

Assurances were also offered that the DLF's operations would parallel private business practices as closely as possible. In one of the earliest official speculations that something more than the EXIM Bank might be necessary, a State Department spokesman expressed confidence that any new institution, "like the RFC and the Export-Import Bank . . . will not lose money."[32] Brand promised that each DLF loan would open "the legitimate possibility of a reasonable profit for somebody, either directly or indirectly."[33]

The Kennedy and Johnson Administrations appeared somewhat more at ease with a government agency playing a role which tradition assigned to private enterprise. Spokesmen tended to speak more frequently of the long-run political and social barriers to private development capital. Yet there was no ceasing in the attempt to weave a picture of new policies with the threads of traditional beliefs. Frank Coffin, Kennedy's appointee as Director of the DLF, reiterated the argument that his agency engaged in a "businesslike, borrower-lender relationship." "To put it another way," he said, "DLF represents the application of proven business practices to some of our economic dealings with other nations."[34]

The greater popularity of the EXIM Bank, as opposed to the DLF, shows that the credo favoring private means of economic development has an autonomy of its own, more or less independent of the self-interest of private investors. The DLF offers benefits to American businesses at least equivalent to those afforded by the EXIM Bank. But EXIM's more acceptable techniques—investment guarantees and loans—merely offer marginal assistance to regular international commercial transactions. DLF activities, on the other hand, involve contracts in which American businessmen are paid directly by the American government for their sales or services abroad.

Policy-makers in the executive, like the public and Congress, have also been concerned with the internal and external behavior of nations receiving foreign aid. The constraints of diplomatic practice tend to make official pronouncements on this subject infrequent and ambiguous. But public statements do demonstrate a desire to have aided nations more ideologically close to the United States in both internal and external policy.

As for internal matters, the chief concern has been with the use of private enterprise for economic development. This is advocated either as axiomatically good because of its expected political and social benefits,[35] or on the basis of the following syllogism: foreign private investment is a good and necessary source of development capital; investors are wary of government competition; therefore governments must prevent or eliminate such competition.[36] To attain this desired American goal, policy spokesmen have not been above criticizing other nations when it is felt that "sound projects are not being planned in which private capital can be used."[37] Nor have they failed to propose with relative candor that American aid resources be used as a "midwife to history" by inducing recipients to embrace acceptable private enterprise techniques: "limited public funds can only supplement and strengthen the efforts of private enterprises and are not available as a substitute for, or to compete with, private enterprise."[38]

Concerning the anticipated international behavior of aid recipients, there has been a marked duality of expressed thought. On the one hand the goal for foreign aid has been repeatedly expressed as a world of free and independent nations. The chief objection to Soviet aid is said to be its attempted use to fashion strong economic and political ties with the nations receiving assistance.[39] On the other hand, much of American policy can be construed as indicating the same intentions as the Soviet Union. We have already noted the hope held out to American business that the results of aid would be closer commercial ties with other nations. The increasing "Buy America" procurement policies in foreign aid are designed to help assure these ties.

As for more general policy orientations, Secretary Dulles' well-known general condemnation of the "immorality" of neutralism is indicative of what has been expected of other nations in their foreign relations. Further evidence of the same sort was supplied by President Eisenhower when he attempted to spell out the difference between American and Russian goals in foreign aid. The result appears as much an exercise in euphemism as a demonstration of any clear distinctions:

> The Soviet Union wants to gain economic, and ultimately political, control of the countries she pretends to help. We, on the other hand, want these countries to stand on their own feet as proud, robust friends and partners.[40]

Despite occasional gestures toward toughness, officials under Kennedy and Johnson have departed somewhat from earlier pronouncements about expected foreign policy behavior. In 1961, for example, President Kennedy made a statement that the United States should favor in its aid programs those nations which "have our view of the world crisis."[41] This statement was consistent with many past expressions of Democratic and Republican Administrations. However, Kennedy himself, and others in the government, subsequently took pains to point out that "our view" meant a desire for a world of viable, independent states. It was a view said to encompass many diverse forms of domestic organization and international behavior.[42]

We can note the difference which time has brought in official statements. In 1950 an official would question merely the speed of Americanization of the world: "Only gradually can [other peoples] adopt our ways. . . ."[43] Some ten years later officials could warn that "what is good for us is not necessarily good for another man," relating this specifically to private vs. public sectors of economic activity.[44] If there still remains a desire to export the American model—in Dean Rusk's words, "we know from experience in our own country how to achieve rapid economic development"[45]—officials now acknowledge that the mere fact of our revolutionary past and the expression of idealistic principles is not enough to make other peoples eager customers for Americanism.[46]

Relations with Congress and the Public

Ideas are only part of politics. The ways ideas are used —the techniques for disseminating them and the skill with which they are propounded—are also important. The problems of philosophical justification for foreign aid are matched by problems of the strategy for securing domestic support.

The frequent reorganizations of the foreign aid administrative apparatus have been noted time and again by journalists and other observers. Almost all commentators decry these changes, some because they say that the formal reorganizations have meant no real alteration in policy; others because of alleged disruptions of policy resulting from frequent administrative revisions. Both arguments have some validity. In spite of the changes certain procedures have persisted relatively unmodified. Yet the shifts in organization have also brought about new styles of operation and new personnel, occasionally with the result of diminished efficiency.

Information liaison has been divided into two categories: contact with the public at large through an office of public information, and contact with Congress through an office of congressional liaison. Under the Agency for International Development, established in 1961, the job of dealing with the public was assigned to the Public Affairs Information Staff (S/PAI). Its organization reflected the Kennedy Administration's policy of bringing greater centralization to foreign aid activities. The functions transferred to S/PAI included those previously performed by the DLF, as well as the public information activities on behalf of foreign aid which were formerly performed by the Department of State. Under subsequent reorganizations the Food for Peace activities were transferred from the White House to the State Department. Food for Peace, assistance to Latin America under the Alliance for Progress, and special projects like Vietnam refugee work all have small public

103

information programs of their own which are coordinated with S/PAI.

The shift to S/PAI of DLF functions was a natural result of administrative consolidation. But the moving of responsibility from the Department of State to the new agency was indicative of a substantive change of public information policy. It was hoped that under the new arrangement a more active and extensive policy of informing the public about foreign aid would be undertaken. The new staff has received an authorized complement of 34 employees, as opposed to 24 positions allocated to foreign aid information activities in the State Department's budget. (Twenty-four was the nominal number working on foreign aid; one official involved in the change-over said there had been trouble finding more than four or five who had been working actively in ICA public information activities.)

Besides expanding its staff, the new organization has developed concepts of public presentations more suited to the specific needs of information about foreign aid. As several officials explained, information policies of the State Department are geared toward the coverage of "spot news," providing background and answering questions about items of current interest to the news media. Furthermore, since many foreign policy decisions do not require specific public and congressional support, the State Department is frequently concerned with disseminating information broadly rather than concentrating on politically important groups or on Congress.

These techniques of public relations were considered inappropriate for foreign aid. A successful aid program requires the consistent support of many groups and institutions outside the executive branch: Congress must provide funds; training facilities must be made available to participants from abroad; skilled personnel must be recruited; business must provide needed commodities and services; and private investment must be stimulated to complement government activities. The three subdivisions of S/PAI—News, Public Services, and

Publications—are expected to adjust information policy to these needs as well as to explain foreign aid on a general basis.

One example of the approach of the S/PAI is indicated by its analysis of a State Department pamphlet entitled "Foreign Aid. Facts and Fallacies." Each section of the pamphlet is headed with a negative statement about foreign aid, with the result that each criticism is given at least as much prominence as the rebuttal. This is particularly striking in the table of contents, which lists all the hostile statements, for example: "We Have Nothing to Show for Our Aid," "Aid Doesn't Win Friends for the United States," and "Foreign Aid Promotes Socialism." As a staff member pointed out, readers may very well remember the arguments against the aid program rather than the refutations.

The goal of the new program has been to recognize these arguments without publicizing them extensively. Stress is placed on what aid is *not*, as a means of parrying criticisms, and the varieties of justifications—idealism, self-interest, and anti-Communism—are discussed in conjunction with one another rather than in isolated sequences. A quotation from an early statement concerning the Alliance for Progress is illustrative:

> It must succeed as D-Day in Normandy had to succeed, and as the Marshall Plan had to succeed—because failure would mean disaster. But it must also succeed as the American Revolution had to succeed—because powerful historical forces propel it.[47]

The Office of Congressional Liaison also underwent changes as a result of the 1961 reorganization. Its size was increased from seven positions under ICA to fourteen under AID. As with S/PAI, the increase in size was but one reflection of a change in attitude toward the functions of the office. The new liaison staff is much more concerned than its predecessor with collecting information about congressional sentiment regarding the program. The staff also represents the program to individual congressmen on a year-round basis rather than only during the time legislation is being considered.

This attempt to "sell" the program is limited, of course, by legal restrictions on executive lobbying and by the known sensitivity of legislators to attempts at pressure by the executive. Yet there are striking differences between the attitudes of those who had served in the old ICA and those in charge of congressional liaison in the new AID concerning what is proper and effective in presenting the program to Congress. One official who had served in this field during the Eisenhower Administration felt that the new operation was clearly in violation of anti-lobbying laws. He insisted that his own role of merely responding to congressional requests for information comprised the full extent of proper behavior. He also felt that there was little use in contacting individual members to present the case for the program. By contrast, one official in the new office succeeded in personally meeting approximately three hundred congressmen within his first year on the job.

Although the offices of public information and congressional liaison are charged with the central responsibility for dealing with groups outside the executive branch, their activities by no means include all the relationships between the agency and relevant publics. They do provide the most useful starting point for studying activities within the agency which affect the strength, composition, and direction of political support for and opposition to foreign aid.

Problems of Gaining Public Support

Simply stated, the basic task of public information activities is to answer two questions: What is going on in the program, and what does the public want to know about it? The task of public information is the same whether it is viewed from the standpoint of providing objective information without regard to its impact upon the public, or from the standpoint from which nearly all public information programs operate—to justify and win approval for certain policies.

For the publicist of foreign aid policies, answering both these questions presents major difficulties. Acquiring information about the program is hampered by a number of procedural and administrative barriers. The simple fact that foreign aid is foreign is one of the most formidable of these barriers. Aid spending in the form of thousands of slowly-developing individual projects occurs in nearly one hundred countries throughout the world. Even without budgetary limits on staff size it would be a monumental task to select the significant information from the mass of contracts, technical plans, construction projects, and other activities which constitute the totality of foreign aid in operation.

Limited personnel resources make the job all the more difficult. Information staffs in both the State Department and AID have used two main sources of information, regular overseas employees, and special information reporters. Both sources are far from perfect. Messages from the field tend to be specialized and technical. There is also a tendency among operational employees to be uninterested in, or actually hostile toward, the need for publicity. Many aid employees fear and reject anything that smacks of "Madison Avenue" in the complicated business of economic development. The problem is compounded by the fact that field employees serve relatively few years in each post. It is rare that the same officials see an aid project from its inception through completion. Thus the identification of the successful school, hospital, or other concrete result of aid spending is rendered all the more difficult.

In the late 1950s attempts were made to supplement the regular channels of information through the use of special reports by the information staff. During the latter years of the ICA a plan was begun to have four regional representatives permanently stationed overseas to write articles and reports about foreign aid activities. However, with the relocation of information activities in AID, this arrangement was abandoned. In its place there was instituted the practice of having Washington-based reporters make periodic trips overseas to gather material.

Several reasons were given for this change. It was felt that the field representatives were in a kind of administrative limbo; they often failed to have sufficiently clear relationships, and hence cooperation, with the State Department, the United States Information Service, and the aid mission. There were also uncertain supervisory links between the home office and work in the field. It was difficult to keep the representatives informed of the changing needs of the information program, and their location abroad made it difficult for them to be continually informed as to the effectiveness of the stories and reports they submitted.

The new arrangement of gathering information through occasional trips is also not without drawbacks. Some officials who had worked under the old system were sharply critical of this part of AID operations. They questioned whether anyone spending a few days or a few weeks in an area could develop the contacts necessary to make observations of sufficient depth and precision to be useful to the agency.

This dilemma of basing means of information-gathering either too far from the source of news or too little integrated with the audience is compounded by an equal difficulty: finding out what the public wants to know.

Although it is administratively better equipped to discern public wishes and uncertainties about foreign aid, the public information office uses many of the same techniques—and encounters many of the same problems—in attempting to identify and analyze its constituency as do members of Congress. The information staff uses essentially the same imprecise indices available to congressmen—letters, editorials, columnists' opinions, and occasional direct contacts with local "opinion leaders."

It frequently uses the inquiries which congressmen themselves relay to the agency from their constituents in order to discern public opinion, though recognizing that the mail is volatile in content, depending upon the shifting tides of current events. Commentary in the mass media, while somewhat more stable, reflects the opinions of only a small, specialized segment of the population, which may or may not be indicative of general opinion.[48] Although opinion studies based on nationwide samples are of potentially greater value to AID than to congressmen, the agency has never regularly gathered polling results.

The strategy of getting information about foreign aid into the channels of public communication follows three principal lines. Through publications and speakers, the public information office attempts to assist local citizens' groups in their study of foreign aid. It also endeavors to publicize stories concerning new personnel or commodity procurement which may have interest in local areas. And it tries to circulate general information about foreign aid policies in the major metropolitan newspapers. Occasionally there is an opportunity for a fourth device, assisting writers in the preparation of technical or feature stories in magazines and journals.

In form these approaches resemble typical governmental information programs. Yet the political context of foreign aid requires certain differences in technique. Most important, there is a scarcity of strong "natural" clientele groups to facilitate communications between the government and the public. Groups that are interested tend to be already firmly committed to aid; they also tend to be weak politically.

Technical problems pose a barrier to efficient communication of home-town news concerning foreign aid. The foreign aid bureaucracy is so large that the procurement of goods and the hiring of personnel are performed by specialized offices. While attempts are made to publicize contracts and purchases in local communities when such information can be obtained in time to make it newsworthy and, whenever possible, meetings are arranged between new employees and their congressmen as a kind of "co-optation" effort to minimize criticism of aid personnel and activities, officials engaged in these endeavors acknowledge their rather hit-or-miss manner of execution. Besides the difficulty of gathering the information necessary for such activities, there is the inhibition against being overly aggressive in information programs involving congressmen.[49]

The principal difficulties elaborated in this chapter —an uncertain rationale for foreign aid and the organizational problems of disseminating effective publicity— further illustrate the political weakness of foreign aid. On the one hand these difficulties indicate the importance of Presidential and other top-level support for the program; on the other hand, they suggest some of the deficiencies in the resources available to win support for foreign aid. Presidential activity in behalf of foreign aid can best be discussed in terms of the political context created by public and congressional reaction to foreign aid. The final chapter will summarize the earlier descriptions of this political context, and will discuss Presidential attempts to work within this context to maximize acceptance of foreign aid.

6

Foreign Aid and the

Political System

The responses of the public and Congress constitute the political environment within which Presidents must work to secure continuation of an acceptable foreign aid policy. Although this environment is frequently characterized by its hostility to foreign aid, its over-all influence is both complex and diverse.

Foreign aid is evaluated by the public according to a series of contrasting and contradictory standards. Aid is favorably received insofar as it appears to project American values or practices abroad, furthers humanitarian aims, avoids deep involvement in the affairs of other nations, and assists cold-war allies. The public and Congress view aid with disfavor to the degree that it offers assistance to nations not allied with the United States, appears to be expensive, and results in deep involvement in overseas problems.

On the whole, survey results have shown slight majorities favoring aid as a general notion. Furthermore,

above average support for aid is found among professionals, white-collar workers, the better educated and
the higher salaried—those groups in society which are
generally the most active and articulate in promoting
their political views. This apparently favorable distribution of opinion is supplemented by the fact that pressure groups supporting foreign aid far outnumber those
opposed. And for the past ten years, most spokesmen
of the two major political parties have endorsed continued American aid activities. There are, as previously
noted, definite anti-aid pressures among the public as
well, but a reading of opinion data would seem to point
to no worse than a balance between pro- and anti-aid
sentiment.

In light of this, it is perplexing, but nevertheless
true, that participants in foreign-aid policy-making—both
congressmen and executive branch officials—normally
perceive public opinion as working against foreign aid
rather than for it. Many congressmen who support aid
policies frankly do so in opposition to the rough indices
of their constituents' opinions; congressional opponents,
on the other hand, freely cite the "demands" of the voters
for their antagonistic positions. From the days of the
Marshall Plan to the present, Presidents and their advisers have felt it necessary to engage in campaigns,
appeals, studies, and reorganizations in the unfulfilled
hope of increasing public support for assistance programs.

Part of the reason for this paradox may be found
in the attitudes from which opinion is formed. While
the aggregate of these attitudes may lead to approval
of aid in principle, there is actually no such thing as
foreign aid "in general." There are instead many alternative means for pursuing specific goals in many disparate
environments throughout the world. Specific aid activities may fall far short of activating positive reactions.
Much aid policy, in fact, conjures up the very images
which create hostile feelings among Americans. Aid to
Communist countries, to unfriendly neutralists, and to
nations with government-controlled economies all clearly

fail to measure up to widely held standards of approval. Even military assistance to allies can provoke latent fears of undesirable long-term commitments. The Peace Corps, which benefits from its low-cost, missionary aura, seems a clear exception which proves the general rule.

Winston Churchill once called democracy the worst form of government—except for all the others that have been tried. The man in the street appears to evaluate foreign aid according to a variant of this aphorism. To the public, foreign aid is a good policy, except for all the forms in which it has been applied.

Predispositions favorable to actual aid policy are found most frequently among those with more than average knowledge of foreign aid and the social and political context within which American policy operates. This knowledge, which may be acquired through education or direct experience, is possessed by relatively few people outside the government. In nongovernmental groups and political parties, individuals with foreign affairs experience often hold positions of leadership and policy-initiation. These are the people who write party platforms, formulate policy resolutions at conventions, and act as group spokesmen in Washington. Because they are found in the two political parties and in a wide variety of interest organizations, their support for foreign aid helps give the appearance of widespread approval which cuts across divisions of party and interest groups. Such approval is not found, however, among the rank-and-file of these organizations. On the whole, members of organizations demonstrate a rather passive antipathy. Leaders are free to differ from followers by supporting aid because the issue fails either to interest or to provoke intense feelings among most citizens.[1] This division on foreign aid is another dimension of the conflict, described by James MacGregor Burns, between the Presidential (or pro-aid), and congressional (or anti-aid), wings of the two national parties.[2]

Sustained approval of foreign aid requires the acceptance of a kind of complex reasoning indulged in by few members of the general public. It is most difficult, therefore, to arouse widespread enthusiasm for the program. On the other hand, the arguments against aid— the "primitive propaganda" against lavishing tax dollars on the reactionary, the corrupt, the unfriendly, or even the Communist—are more likely to tap the emotions of the mass public, inducing them to write letters or otherwise articulate their feelings.[3]

There is a second major characteristic of the political climate of foreign aid. Although the means by which opinion is normally channeled to the government—such as party or group activity—appear to be relatively ineffective, and although legislative and executive branch officials are themselves frequently uncertain of the nature of public opinion, the beliefs and assumptions found in public thinking are nevertheless prominent in both the legislative and executive stages of policy-making.[4]

We have already noted that these premises may lead to unfavorable attitudes toward aid. But, as indicated in the last chapter, the governmental proponents of aid have for the most part accepted the traditional positions and used them in attempting to secure support for aid policy. In essence, the advocates of aid ask: How can the benefits of free enterprise and other aspects of American society be transmitted abroad unless active steps are taken to facilitate this transmission? How can we maintain an alliance system against a powerful adversary unless we assist our allies to build their own soundly-based defense establishments? How can we expect other nations to take our side in the cold war unless we take their side in the struggle for development? Why should we be content with a defensive ring around our homeland when we have the opportunity to construct such a ring around our enemies? To critics who question the feasibility of these objectives, the proponents answer that it takes time. The Kennedy Administration's "Decade of Development" was a prime example of a traditionalist pro-aid answer to traditionalist anti-aid argument.

Presidents and their advisers have done more than

advance philosophical arguments, of course, in attempting to increase support for aid. Given the technical problems of conducting an effective information program plus the absence of a favorable political climate, executive branch leaders have taken steps designed to increase the legitimacy, or general acceptability, of foreign aid.

Beginning with the European Recovery Program, planning in the executive branch has included consideration of how foreign aid might be presented to the public most effectively. Even before an affirmative decision on assistance to Europe had been finally reached in the State Department it was suggested that a desirable predecisional step might be to send a delegation of prominent Americans to survey the problems of war-shattered Europe.[5] Presumably such a group would be useful in simultaneously "informing" both the government and the public of the need for American assistance. In late 1947, after Secretary of State Marshall's speech proposing aid to Europe, a public "Committee for the Marshall Plan" was organized to encourage public support and direct it into the most useful political channels.[6] The Committee advertised itself in newspapers throughout the country, organized state and city subcommittees, sponsored innumerable speeches on radio and before public groups, and distributed over a million pieces of literature. The Committee's work was timed to reach a high point during the critical phases of congressional treatment of the Marshall Plan legislation. Since that time planners in the White House and elsewhere in the executive branch have periodically endeavored to revive the successes of the Marshall Plan Committee.

The organization and operations of the Committee have, in fact, remained a model for more recent attempts to rally public support for foreign aid. Although nothing as comprehensive as the first committee has been organized in recent years, Presidents and their advisers have nevertheless given much time to special meetings of public-minded citizens on issues of economic development and to public groups supporting American as-

sistance policies. Between 1959 and 1963, five special
studies of foreign aid were requested by the President:
The Draper Committee; the Kennedy Task Force on
Foreign Aid, headed by Henry R. Labouisse; a report
by Senator Mike Mansfield (D., Mont.); the Clay Committee Report; and a study by Under Secretary of State
George Ball ordered by President Johnson. The findings
of all but the last of these have been made public.[7]
Many of these studies, meetings, and other actions are
superficially diverse, but they share one significant feature: they are widely used and generally effective in
the launching of new political programs, but they frequently lead to unintended negative consequences when
applied to policies already in effect.

This holds true for general statements of Presidential
support for foreign aid as well as the more elaborate
campaigns to promote public enthusiasm. These statements of support are undoubtedly a positive asset for
foreign aid because of the general willingness by Congress and the public to accept Presidential freedom of
action in conducting foreign relations.[8] Presidents Truman, Eisenhower, Kennedy, and Johnson have all expressed their desire for a strong foreign aid program.
Experienced officials have placed Presidential support
near the top of the list of resources helpful in eliciting
such favorable response as the program does receive. Yet
the overlay of bureaucracy and money needed to carry
out the program, and its continuation without clear-cut
results, has necessitated frequent reaffirmation of Presidential support, often in terms of alleged emergency
conditions. Occasionally the cry of emergency is per-
suasive and leads to relative success, as with the Marshall
Plan, the special assistance to Latin America in 1960–
1961 (for which the full executive branch requests were
appropriated), or with the removal of specific restrictions in the aid legislation. But more often critics can
accuse the executive of crying "crisis" and "anti-communism" so often as to erode the credibility of such
appeals. The effectiveness of these appeals is further

weakened by the fact that it is possible to make substantial decreases in funds and to add many far-reaching restrictions while still passing the program. Presidential determinations of "vital security needs" cannot easily be seen to apply to specific percentages of fund requests or many of the operational requirements imposed by Congress.

Presidents have justified their support for the program in numerous ways. The frequent reorganization and re-naming of the foreign aid agency are partly responses to changing ideas as to how aid policy should be conducted. But these administrative modifications are also in large measure designed to indicate that the President and his advisers are keeping a close watch on the program. The substitution of the International Cooperation Administration for the Foreign Operations Administration was specifically defended by President Eisenhower in terms of its impact on the public.[9] While the change from ICA to AID was not justified in explicit public relations terms, it was closely linked with the attempt of the Kennedy Administration to project the image of revitalizing the foreign aid program.[10]

The attempt to give the appearance of concern, change, and improvement has resulted in the creation of eight successive foreign aid agencies—from the Marshall Plan's Economic Cooperation Administration in 1948 to the establishment of AID in 1961—an average of better than one new agency every two years. Accompanying the rapid turnover of agencies is an even more rapid turnover of aid administrators. In this same period there were ten administrators, each with an average tenure of eighteen months. France's Fourth Republic could scarcely outdo this record of leadership shuffling.

These repeated "hard looks" at foreign aid, especially by incoming administrators, have come to be accepted as mere ritual by both friends and foes of foreign aid. Their contribution to the enhancement of public support for the program appears minimal. The irony here is that while the intent has been to give the appearance of Presidential concern with foreign aid efficiency, the frequent inquiries, the restructuring, and the shuffling of personnel have had the clear effect of making the aid program less efficient, less able to perform according to the high standards expected of it. Several aid administrators, for example, were selected more for the purposes of public image than for competence in the field of foreign aid. In at least one case (John Hollister, an Eisenhower appointee) the administrator's chief asset seemed to be his conspicuous lack of sympathy for foreign aid.

Dr. D. A. FitzGerald, for fifteen years the highest permanent foreign aid official, has sharply rebuked both Republican and Democratic Administrations for these practices. After his retirement in 1962, he complained of the "farcical game of musical chairs" to which the program was repeatedly subjected. Noting that it generally took a year before an aid official could become "reasonably effective," he pointed out the obvious consequences for agency efficiency resulting from the rapid turnover of top officials. Furthermore, he said, the frequent top-to-bottom reorganizations were extremely harmful to morale within the agency. He was highly critical of the tendency to "disparage programs and performances of the past," despite the fact that "no brand-new principles have been discovered and put into effect." Dr. FitzGerald claimed that the "periodic attempts to shuck off the old and don the new" have the far-reaching consequences of breeding a lack of public and congressional confidence in the integrity of the program.[11]

The use of citizen study-groups and public conferences as a means of expressing high-level concern with the program parallels the uses of reorganization. Generally speaking, the results of using these groups have been less tangible than has been the case with reorganizations, but there is little evidence that they have been any more useful, either in legitimizing foreign aid or in bringing about actual improvements in policy.

118

Indeed, it is possible to identify results neither expected nor desired by the sponsors of such studies. One extreme case is the Report of the Clay Committee, in 1963, which helped bolster the arguments of congressmen who wanted to cut aid funds and add administrative restrictions.[12] One official has noted the feeling that perhaps foreign aid's most notable achievement is to have survived all the study groups which have beset it.[13]

This use of citizen-groups in the search for general support should be distinguished from their more limited and specific employment which has met with greater success. The study of the use of cooperatives in overseas economic development has been associated with support for foreign aid by the American cooperative movement.[14] And public support for a controversial loan to Ghana was increased after a favorable report on the loan was issued by a study group headed by industrialist Clarence B. Randell.[15]

In many ways, and at many points in the making of policy, the process described by Gunnar Myrdal as "the law of cumulative causation" appears to work to the disadvantage of attempts to increase public support for foreign aid. The lack of widespread interest in foreign aid makes difficult the task of communicating effectively with the public; the general political vulnerability of the program raises legal and psychological barriers to aggressive information programs which might overcome public indifference and antipathy. Through frequent repetition, attempts to demonstrate innovation and improvement result in public cynicism and operational disorder. The very complexity of the program leads both to low levels of public understanding and to difficulties in assembling and effectively presenting information to the public.

These conditions can be more clearly observed by comparing them with the sharply contrasting situation of the Peace Corps. The philosophical advantages of this new program have already been pointed out. It also possesses positive strengths in the very areas where AID has been weak. The relatively small size of the Peace Corps permits close relations between operations and publicity. It conducts projects which permit individuals to end their service after only two years, so that constant recruitment is made from many occupational groups of the population. Channels of communication can be established which permit a combination of recruitment and general favorable publicity cast in terms of the interests of doctors, lawyers, nurses, teachers, and other groups. In addition, the fact that it has been accepted as a "public service" client of the Advertising Council permits its message to be prominently and frequently disseminated through nearly all forms of mass media from subway posters to radio and television.

It was for these very good publicity reasons that the Peace Corps was not brought within the administrative framework of AID, despite the general desire for greater consolidation of foreign-assistance activities by many in the Kennedy Administration. Fragmentation won the day in order to preserve the unique favorable image of this new aid endeavor.[16] This may be another instance in which the desire to project a favorable public image results in at least the possibility of less effective policy. Some operating officials have questioned whether short-term employment (of both volunteers and staff) which gives the impression of freshness is really in the long-run best interests of the goals of economic development. There is further doubt whether the Peace Corps is concentrating sufficiently on building the foundations for long-range institutions necessary for sustaining economic and social development. Operating officials in AID have also been concerned about the increased burdens of coordination placed on higher-level foreign policy officials as a result of the Peace Corps' independent existence.

Within the system of congressional-executive relations are represented many of the features of the politics of foreign aid which have been outlined in the preceding pages. These features add up to a situation in a kind of tenuous equilibrium, resulting not from consensus among the participants but from the inability of Congress and the executive either to avoid engaging in this particular policy conflict or to convince each other to accept its own preferences. The executive must participate in this conflict because it needs financial and general support for the program. Congress must participate because of its acknowledged obligation to give at least some assent to serious, persistent requests by the President in the realm of foreign policy.

The strength of conflicting positions stems in each case from a number of sources—the proportion of appealing and repelling components in the aid program submitted to Congress; the uncertainty toward aid fostered by political attitudes based essentially on domestic questions; and the kinds of political tools available to the executive.

The Peace Corps was cited above as one element of foreign aid which stimulated unqualified positive responses. The philosophical ambiguity of other parts of the aid program has also been noted. Military aid, for example, represents a clear and concrete response to an international threat, but it is also among the most expensive components of aid, and it carries with it the threat of relatively costly commitment in the event of violence abroad. In recent years it has also come to be associated with supporting autocratic, nonprogressive foreign regimes. The ambiguity of congressional reactions to military assistance can be noted from the following observations: only on the question of military aid have the decisions of the Appropriations Committee to reduce funds been modified by the full House of Representatives since 1958—on two occasions the House abandoned its habitual deference to committees and increased the military appropriations. On the other hand, during the same period military funds ranked fifth in percentage of total requests finally appropriated among seven identifiable categories of foreign aid appropriations.

Other segments of the aid program contain similar features likely to provoke mixed reactions. Technical assistance benefits from being seen as an extension of American "know-how" abroad; but it is also a grant program and thus suffers from the pervasive concern about cost. The Development Loan Fund has the advantage of engaging in programs which result in dollar repayments to the United States; but it is the most costly nonmilitary component, and its administration requires a relatively large amount of autonomy from Congress. The long-range commitments involved in granting DLF funds have also been a factor inhibiting support. This fear of commitments was said to be a chief cause for congressional disapproval of a proposed long-term plan to assist the construction of a steel production complex in Bokaro, India.[17]

Some estimates of the relative advantages and disadvantages of the various segments of foreign aid legislation can be seen in Figure VI-1. The segments were ranked horizontally according to the amount of money requested. They were ranked vertically according to the percentage of requests finally appropriated. The general importance of cost is apparent. Three of the legislative categories—technical assistance, administrative expenses, and United Nations technical assistance—exhibit a precise negative correlation between total amount requested and percentage of each amount finally approved. There are two pairs of aid funds which deviate from this correlation. The DLF and the President's Contingency Fund received larger fund cuts than would be expected from the size of the spending requests. Military assistance and Supporting Assistance (which helps compensate for allies' defense spending) received relatively smaller fund reductions. These two departures are consistent with the inferences previously made about the values used in judging different parts of foreign aid. The DLF and the Contingency Fund suffer from the absence of congressional control in their allocation. The DLF also meets with disapproval because it represents a high

Figure VI-1. RELATIONSHIP BETWEEN SIZE OF APPROPRIATION REQUEST AND PERCENTAGE OF REQUEST FINALLY APPROPRIATED, FISCAL YEARS 1958–1963

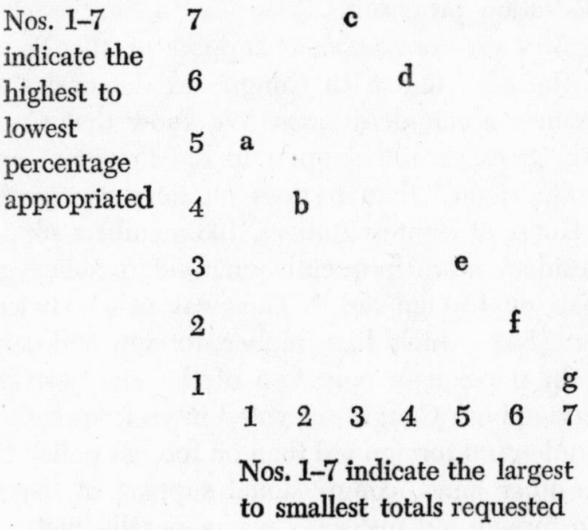

Nos. 1–7 indicate the highest to lowest percentage appropriated

```
7              c
6                   d
5   a
4       b
3                e
2                       f
1                           g
    1   2   3   4   5   6   7
```

Nos. 1–7 indicate the largest to smallest totals requested

a Military aid	e Technical Assistance
b Defense Support	f Administrative Funds
c Development Loan Fund	g U.N. Technical
d Contingency Fund	Assistance

degree of American involvement in the long, slow process of foreign economic development. Military aid, on the other hand, has benefited from its association with the exigencies of cold-war crises.[18]

Part of the difficulty facing the executive branch in attempting to win congressional support for foreign aid arises from a problem of definitions. The executive has been unable to win full acceptance of its definition of foreign aid as a foreign policy question, which would imply a high degree of congressional compliance with executive requests. We have already seen how the public, pressure groups, and Congress tend to react to foreign aid in terms of domestic standards and expectations associated with foreign aid. Thus, concern with questions of spending (both as to amount and allocation), congressional supervision of administration, and the transmittal of domestic norms and values overseas permit the congressmen wide latitude in questioning and amending Administration proposals.

Figures on congressional support of the President during the 86th and 87th Congresses demonstrate this ambivalence about definitions. We know that Congress normally gives greater support to the President on foreign policy issues than it does on domestic questions. In the House of Representatives, 108 members supported the President more frequently on foreign policy generally than on foreign aid.[19] This was nearly twice the number (58) which had higher foreign aid support scores. In the Senate only two of the eighty-six members serving both Congresses voted more frequently with the President on foreign aid than on foreign policy issues. On the other hand, congressional support of the President on foreign aid measures was generally higher during the same period than support on domestic policy measures.

The application of domestic criteria to foreign-aid decisions helps explain periodic "liberal revolts" against the program. These occur when traditional supporters of aid programs (especially under Kennedy and Johnson) protest the lack of concern for how well recipient governments adhere to standards of liberal democracy at home and the American view of the cold war abroad. These defections are important not only because of the loss of individual votes but also because of the loss of prestige which occurs within and without Congress when a program is attacked by members from whom support is normally forthcoming.

The executive has been frustrated in trying to cope with these objections. Altering the program in the direction desired by the liberals is unlikely to please conservatives who may not share the same vision of the good society. Executive officials have also become less willing (or less confident of their capacity) to demand

high levels of international conformity from other nations
as the price for receiving aid.

The executive is further hampered in its quest for
political support by the fact that while it has the "big
guns" of Presidential prestige in dealing with Congress,
it has available few of the more refined tools of political
barter. Some concessions to congressional patronage interests are undoubtedly made in hiring. But most positions available have such precise technical requirements
that there is little opportunity to permit significant compliance with the demands of patronage. Likewise the
several billions of dollars spent annually in the United
States are of little use for legislative bargaining. As one
congressional liaison official said: "We'd sure as hell
like to use the money, but the allocation system is too
complicated and slow to be any good to us." The long
process by which projects are approved, and contractors
and sellers located (often through competitive bidding)
places most aid spending beyond the use of manipulation
for congressional support.[20]

Furthermore, most techniques of executive-legisla-
tive bargaining are effectively employed only "at the
margin"—when legislative consensus is uncertain or divided. Until 1963, the chief opponent of foreign aid,
Congressman Passman, was so well entrenched in his
subcommittee that attempts at political persuasion were
a waste of time. With the accession of a new Appropriations Committee Chairman more favorable to aid, the
balance in the committee became uncertain. At this point
it became politically profitable for executive officials to
seek favorable votes from "swing members" on the subcommittee.

Furthermore, techniques used to build support for
policy in one political context may be ineffective under
other conditions. Defense projects, public works, and
many social welfare activities generally lead to approval
from those who come in direct contact with them. Where
general understanding and support for a program is lacking, as with foreign aid, such direct contact may not

have favorable effects. An example is the Warner and Swasey Company of Cleveland, Ohio, which placed an advertisement in the April 23, 1962, issue of *U.S. News and World Report*, sharply condemning foreign aid.[21] The message was entitled, "No Wonder We're Broke!" It presumably referred to the United States, and not the company itself, which had sales to the foreign aid program averaging nearly $30,000 per year between 1954 and 1962.[22]

The policy-making system, while not completely the "empty ritual" that some have called it, has certainly been an unsatisfying ritual from the standpoint of both Congress and the executive. Congress feels constrained to approve each year a piece of major legislation whose goals are ambiguous, whose means are suspect, and the past application of which is characterized by well-published examples of alleged incompetency and dishonesty. Congressmen have had little opportunity to find an acceptable middle ground between the fears of tomorrow and the hopes of the day after tomorrow with which the executive advocates its position, as opposed to the sweeping allegations of wrong-doing with which opponents argue for the abandonment of foreign aid.

The substance of debate has often turned upon the most recent and often transitory events concerning aid which have caught the attention of Congress and the public: the question of expropriation and the rights of foreign investment abroad, the mixture of American and Russian funds in the same aid projects, aid to Communist governments, the support of dictators, aid to those who trade with Communists, and assistance to those nations (such as Egypt) which use discriminatory policies in barring ships from international waterways. These issues periodically crop up as topics for concern, with little sustained attention or progress toward resolution.

Further, the acts of Congress in trying to place philosophically satisfying restrictions on the program often lead to the very situations least desired by legislators. In recent years Congress has made grand gestures against aid to Communists, countries which trade with Communists, or aid to nations which discriminate in international waterways. In each case, however, the gesture was accompanied by a provision permitting the President to waive the legislative restrictions. Congress thus formally delegated more discretion to the President while decrying the growth of executive power at the expense of the legislature.

For its part the executive has annually received authority to conduct foreign aid. But it has received this authority only at the expense of great amounts of time, effort, and personal harassment. Its representatives must prepare lengthy presentation documents to Congress, appear at hearings (which may continue for weeks and last up to twelve hours a day), and respond rapidly to detailed congressional inquiries. The administration of aid is also complicated by the restrictions—changed almost annually—as to who may and may not receive money, the general criteria to be used in providing aid, and the precise details of allocating assistance.

Starting from an uncertain philosophical base, and faced with shifting congressional concerns, the executive has often resorted to the simplified appeal and the exaggerated claim for past successes and future dangers. The 1961 debate concerning placing the DLF on long-term financing well illustrates these general points. The motives of the Administration as stated privately and publicly were so unclear that various congressmen were prompted to announce their opposition for reasons which were nearly in direct contradiction to one another. Some decried what they saw as an attempt by the executive to bypass Congress completely and thus destroy the constitutional balance of the separation of powers. Others said they could see no reason to support the change since the executive, in emphasizing the congressional controls which would still remain, was in effect saying that its plan would result in no change at all.

In floor debate and elsewhere Administration spokesmen invoked the dangers of Congress' cutting off important foreign projects during their five-year (or longer) construction period, with immeasurable harm to American foreign policy. Upon questioning, it was admitted that this was only a possibility, and that Congress had never actually done this. Opponents of the new policy placed the most unfavorable light on likely executive actions in the event of the plan's approval. They were sure that officials would commit five years' worth of funds in one or two years, and ignore congressional wishes until they returned for more money, pleading grave new emergencies.[23]

The polarization of the debate was matched by the uncertainty of the outcome. The borrowing authority was not approved. Yet the President called the result a "wholly acceptable compromise."[24] Many officials did feel that the resulting legislation, which provided long-term authorization with annual appropriation, was something they could live with. But others on Capitol Hill who had fought strenuously for the President's original plan felt let down by the easy acceptance of the result; as one staff member said in an interview, "We would think a long time before working this hard for the Administration again."

Foreign Aid Politics in Perspective

The twenty-year record of postwar American foreign aid policy is sufficiently vast and complex to provide the observer with evidence for almost any verdict he desires. Presidents have shown great vision—or intolerable profligacy—in requesting $4 billion per year for foreign assistance. Likewise, Congress has been prompted by fiscal prudence—or selfish misanthropy—in cutting some $800 million from the annual requests. Judgment of American performance depends upon a baffling calculus whose equations are themselves composed of virtual imponderables: What are the tolerable limits of government spending? What mixtures of American money, material, and services are appropriate for the problems of under-developed countries? How much outside assistance can be profitably used by these countries? Just what overseas political and economic consequences must be achieved before American aid may be judged successful? Many observers take satisfaction in answering these questions with absolute doctrines. But the quantity of our dogma far outstrips the certainty of our knowledge; the apparent assurance with which these matters are analyzed is less a testament to our wisdom than to our capacity for generating unwarranted self-confidence.[25]

But if it is premature to make definitive assessments about the performance of the American people and government abroad, we can at least draw some limited conclusions about the postwar record. Perhaps the most noteworthy fact is that there is an American foreign aid program at all. The American past provides but fragile precedents for the rather daring international experiments in which we are currently engaged. Americans are noted for their cycles of isolationism and aggressive interventionism; for their tendency to be impatient at the course of international diplomacy; for their suspicion of political dealings with foreigners; and for their great resistance to government spending on risky or ambiguous projects —all attitudes which have had to be minimized to allow even tolerance for foreign aid.

American political leaders have been accused, not without reason, of seeking political gain with anti-foreign, jingoistic appeals to the public. Yet Harry Truman matched toughness toward the Russians with economic aid to other nations; anti-American outbursts induced the Eisenhower Administration to be more responsive to Latin American requests for economic assistance; John F. Kennedy (who had, as a Senator, urged more liberal aid policies upon the Eisenhower Administration) successfully campaigned on the argument that the Republicans had not done enough in aid and other fields; and the most recent of the jingoist candidates, Barry Goldwater, led his party into an electoral slaughter of such magnitude as to preclude for the foreseeable future his hard-line nationalist strategy in fashioning foreign policy issues.

Even Congress, the well-known enemy of foreign aid, has not failed to make its contributions to the program. Its demands for increased assurance that projects are technically worthy, while in some degree a petulant and futile search for perfection, have nevertheless at times required both the American and recipient governments to make better use of aid funds. Congressional friends of foreign aid often have provided the initial impulses for translating the vast aid program into comprehensible packages. The Johnson Administration's plans for an executive service corps, to provide expanded agricultural assistance, international education, and international health programs are all in this tradition. Such programs are likely to benefit politically by appealing to Americans for whom "foreign aid" is an impossibly opaque policy, but who favor government action in public administration, agriculture, education, health, or other specific fields.

Proponents of aid may also take satisfaction in the degree to which Congressman Passman has suffered a decline in influence. The accession of Congressman George Mahon as Chairman of the Appropriations Committee, and the election of a strongly pro-aid 88th Congress in the wake of the Johnson-Goldwater Presidential campaign, led to an appropriation for Fiscal Year 1965 which was an unprecedented 92.4 per cent of executive branch requests.

Yet the aid picture is far from unblemished. The opponents of aid may have failed in trimming the program to their liking, but they have succeeded in injecting what Theodore White has called a "mechanical orthodoxy" into the foreign aid debate.[26] Proponents advocate aid by invoking unattainable goals. Opponents note how distant the goals remain, and attack not the objectives but the means by which the goals are sought.[27] The temptation remains overwhelming to continue appeals directed toward the lowest common denominator of understanding—such as anti-communism or the export of Americanism. Many have felt that modifying the appeals, let alone the substance of the program, would be to play directly into the hands of the critics.

Too many questions remain concerning the present and future courses of foreign aid to allow any confident conclusion that American politics have come to terms with the external world in which foreign aid is applied. And it is quite proper for the Congress and the public to continue pressing these questions. A "realistic" foreign aid program, purged of all philosophical content, dealing only with short-run international bargaining and attempts at influence, is probably neither possible nor desirable. America is giving of itself in foreign aid, and it is quite natural to expect something in return. However, trying to restrict aid to that which is in the "national interest" is no more a useful guide to policy than the simplistic assumptions about transforming foreign culture into the American image. We have no more consensus about what the "national interest" is in these matters than we do about what aspects of "Americanism" we should try to export. Both issues are vitally in need of debate.

Some hard national introspection seems in order. What are the best of American values? How much of our culture is exportable? How rapidly should we expect the diffusion of values? What degree of compliance with our wishes by others is really necessary for our national security, as opposed to our national ego?

How seriously do we believe in our frequently-invoked pragmatism—enlarging those activities that produce desirable results and abandoning policies which do not? Many of the current aid practices may be seriously challenged from this standpoint. The preference for loans over grants is comprehensible in terms of American values which favor "sound," "business-like" foreign aid. But in terms of achieving the greatest development per dollar spent, loans may be much inferior to grants, since they burden recipients with an obligation to allocate an ever-increasing fraction of their national budgets for debt payment rather than internal growth. The presumed discipline injected into the aid program by loans is illusory; whether foreign aid is a grant or a loan is wholly irrelevant in most of the operations by which resources are transferred.[28] Government officials have admitted that loan repayments prolong the period for which nations will be dependent upon aid;[29] but because of genuine beliefs or fear of Congress, officials continue to rely upon loans for a large share of economic aid.

Senator J. William Fulbright and others have questioned the pragmatism of our policy in another area, claiming that the logic of our goals in foreign aid requires a much greater dose of multilateral aid at the expense of bilateral policies. Multilateral aid, so the argument goes, promotes development more efficiently per dollar of aid, and eliminates the undesirable patron-client relationship which is generated under current practices. If we seriously value pluralism as a goal and pragmatism as a means, present bilateral policies may be dangerously counterproductive.

An underlying problem which exacerbates all these issues is the failure to make, and stick with, a decision as to whether development, as such, is to be the goal of foreign aid. Although development (a difficult concept in itself) has been the nominal purpose for which funds have been spent, it has long been clear that no one involved in policy-making has actually been satisfied with such a modest goal. Development and anti-communism; development and military alliance; development and liberal democracy; development and a capitalist economy; development and social justice; development and pro-Americanism—the embellishments differ from speaker to speaker but they are always supplied, they are always presumed to flow "naturally" from development, and they have always been a source of criticism of foreign aid when development does not lead to the additional objectives desired.

It is true that many of these secondary objectives are important in themselves; it is likewise true that development may from time to time help promote some of these objectives; but it is most certainly true that development cannot lead to all of them in all countries. A fundamental question in foreign aid, then, is the matter of priorities: Is development itself an adequate goal for foreign aid? Can Americans live with the occasional unpleasant consequences of development, relying on techniques perhaps more appropriate than foreign aid to counter these unpleasant results and to maximize the more desirable consequences?

Such limiting of the purpose of foreign aid may seem to be denigrating the concept. And it may prove harmful to public support for the program. As the Peace Corps shows, the only really politically successful programs are those for which the public can generate some enthusiastic emotion. But such limiting may also be a step in closing the gap between what is expected of foreign aid and the means to fulfill these expectations. The historical record shows that with skill, enough resources—and luck—foreign aid can occasionally help promote increased per capita income, progressive social change, or other aspects of development. Much of the dissatisfaction with the program stems from its inability to achieve other purposes. One might well ask whether we have not programmed failure into foreign aid by demanding that it do things for which it has neither the quantitative nor qualitative resources.

Cataloguing these unanswered questions and unresolved issues is an unsatisfactory, but realistic, way to conclude this study. If this overview of the American response to foreign aid has shown anything, it is that for all the billions of dollars spent, for all the countless words uttered, for all the actual achievements attained, the American view of foreign aid remains at an astonishingly primitive level. There is a truly remarkable gap between the potential of foreign aid, the practice of foreign aid, and the rhetoric with which aid is discussed. From one perspective the United States has, in a tangle of necessity and design, embarked upon the unique international experiment of genuine international problem-solving to eliminate the physical deprivation which has been the lot of the majority of mankind since the dawn of history. From another perspective this country has merely reacted to a series of short-run problems with the minimum of insight or planning. The Marshall Plan, now viewed as a kind of "golden age" of foreign aid, wedded remembrances of post-World War I instability with current fears of Communist expansion; it was largely a finesse which succeeded. President Truman's much-lauded Point Four Program was essentially a last-minute public relations gesture designed to enliven an otherwise uninspired inaugural address.[30] Its implications were apparently given very little consideration before being announced to the world—and to the Department of State, where it was received with surprise, hostility, or both (the reports vary).[31] One looks in vain at present for signs that the challenge and response within the political system are producing a clearer vision of where we are going or, indeed, where we now stand with regard to foreign aid. Even President Johnson's widely advertised power to perform legislative miracles has had little impact in resolving doubts about the program. He scored some statistical successes in minimizing budgetary reductions as the bill went through Congress. But much of his achievement was caused by the unprecedented, and temporary, large liberal majority in the 89th Congress, elected in the course of the monumental Republican defeat in 1964. Even this 89th Congress, in its second session, revived the habit of cutting aid funds sharply, adding numerous administrative restrictions, and seriously questioning the basic premises on which the aid program was organized. That the impetus for these attacks came from the normally friendly Senate, rather than from the House, merely indicates the depth of doubt and hostility which the program attracts.

Clarification of these doubts is certainly not the responsibility of any one leader, any one part of the government, any one political party, any one faction of the American people. The material and philosophical demands upon society are too great, and the opportunities for accomplishment too broad, to permit a narrowly-based view of foreign aid. Reconciling foreign aid activities, if they can, in fact, be reconciled, with traditional notions of national interest and evolving judgments of national purpose requires fundamental decisions which can be reached in the only way democracies know how —by the continuing challenge and debate of all those who care.

Appendix

The Ranking of Values with

Respect to Foreign Aid

This analysis of public opinion poll data is based on the following assumptions: (1) Certain questions asked in polls bring out two identifiable aspects of opinion about foreign aid, as described in Chapter 2. (2) Responses to such questions demonstrate the effect on opinion of certain combinations of elements in foreign aid programs. (3) By comparing the results of two or more questions which have one element in common it is possible to rank the strengths of positive and negative factors relative to foreign aid. (4) Such results can be compared with one another over a maximum period of about fifteen years and irrespective of the particular random sample of the population queried. This assumption is supported by the general stability of responses to the same question over time. (See Chapter 2.) (5) The theoretical "base point" of public opinion on foreign aid is a 50-50 split between favorable and unfavorable opinion (excluding those without opinions). This assumption stems from the fact that the general question on foreign aid, as asked by the AIPO, has received favorable responses of about 50 per cent. (See Chapter 2.) The relative strength of positive and negative factors can be estimated by the extent to which responses to poll questions depart from this even division. The conjunction of equally weighted positive and negative factors will result in an even division of opinion.

Identifying the components in each question was in some respects arbitrary. (The terms used are from Chapter 2.) Economic aid and technical assistance were considered non-entangling, especially when proposed in conjunction with the threat of Communist aggression. Military aid was judged to imply deep involvement in all cases. The recipients of aid were coded as non-allies unless the fact of alliance was explicit in the question or, in the early postwar surveys, when a wartime ally such as Great Britain was named.

Listed below are the questions used in this analysis, the dates when asked, the percentages (averaged where necessary) of positive reactions, and the elements of the opinion climate held to be encompassed by the question. (All questions are from National Opinion Research Center, *American Programs of Foreign Aid,* February 1957, processed.)

1. "People who think they've found out why the League of Nations failed are now preparing for a new union of nations, if we win the war. Nobody can say for sure whether a new union would end all wars or only lead to worse ones. In order to try out a union of nations as a possible way of preventing war, would you yourself be willing or not willing to stay on a rationing system in this country for about five years to help feed the starving people in other countries?"

(Asked in January and June 1943. Average rate of approval, 84 per cent. Categorized as "humanitarianism/high cost.")

2(a). "As you may know, the United States has been sending economic aid—like machinery and supplies —to countries that have agreed to stand with us against Communist aggression. Do you think we should continue to send economic aid to these countries, or not?"

(b). "Do you think we should or should not continue to send economic aid—like machinery and supplies —to countries that have agreed to stand with us against Communist aggression?"

(These two questions were asked a total of five times from January 1955 to November 1956. Average rate of approval, 83 per cent. Questions categorized as "low involvement/allies.")

3. "Do you think the United States should continue to give relief to the people in European countries that were occupied by the enemy—such as France and Greece?"

(Asked in October 1945. Rate of approval, 82 per cent. Categorized as "humanitarianism/allies.")

4. "In general do you think it is a good policy for the United States to try to help backward countries in the world to raise their standard of living or shouldn't this be any concern of our government?"

(Asked seven times from March 1949 to March 1955. Average rate of approval, 72 per cent. Categorized as "ideological/non-allies.")

5(a). "Do you approve or disapprove of the United States sending military supplies to the countries of Western Europe now, in order to strengthen them against any future attack?"

(b). "Do you approve or disapprove of sending military supplies to the countries of Western Europe?"

(These two questions were asked twelve times from July 1950 to November 1956. Average rate of approval, 70 per cent. Categorized as "deep involvement/allies.")

6(a). "Some people say we should not send food or relief to countries where the governments say or do unfriendly things to the United States. Others say we should help those that really need it, even if their present governments are unfriendly to us." (Respondents were asked for their opinion on this matter.)

(b). "As you may know, many people in India are starving now, and their government has asked us for help. Do you approve of the United States giving food to them, even though India opposes our policy in Korea?"

(These two questions were asked in February 1947 and April 1951. Average rate of approval, 54 per cent. Categorized as "humanitarianism/non-allies.")

7. "We have also sent economic aid to some countries like India, which have *not* joined us as allies against the Communists. Do you think we should continue to send economic aid to these countries or not?"

(Asked six times between January and December 1956. Average rate of approval, 49 per cent. Categorized as "low involvement/non-allies.")

8. "As you know, some of our allies are asking for loans from the United States in order to get back on their feet. If we made a loan of several billion dollars to England, do you think they would pay us back in full, or in part, or not at all? How about Russia? China? Would you approve or disapprove of making such a loan to England? Russia? China?

(Asked October 1945. Average approval of a loan for all three countries, 45 per cent. Categorized as "allies/high cost.")

A figure showing the results of the associations of these values appears on page 140.

On the basis of this figure we can make the following comparisons regarding the relative strength of the positive values: ideological > humanitarianism; humanitarianism = low involvement; and humanitarianism > allies. Thus we can begin to construct the list which appears in Chapter 2:

> Ideological
> Humanitarianism; Low involvement
> Allies

The relative strengths of the negative factors are compiled as follows: non-allies > high cost; high cost > deep involvement. Therefore:

> Non-allies
> High Cost
> Deep involvement

INTERACTION OF VALUES IN OPINION ON FOREIGN AID

	Allies						
Ideological	*	Ideological					
Low Cost	*	*	Low Cost				
Humanitarianism	82	*	*	Humanitarianism			
Low Involvement	83	*	*	*	Low Involvement		
Non-Allies	*	72	*	54	49	Non-Allies	
High Cost	45	*	*	84	*	*	High Cost
Deep Involvement	70	*	*	*	*	*	*

* No figure available.

We also know from the figure that low involvement + non-allies = 0. (That is, the positive strength of low involvement is equal to the negative strength of non-allies.) Similarly, allies + high cost = 0. This permits us to estimate the relative positions of the two lists:

Positive	*Negative*
Ideological	—
Humanitarianism;	
low involvement	Non-allies
Allies	High cost
—	Deep involvement

Computation also shows that whatever difficulties are involved in the assumptions of this analysis, it is internally consistent. The list shows that humanitarianism + non-allies = 0, which is empirically supported in the "humanitarianism/non-allies" question, which has an approval figure of 54 per cent, closely approximating the expected balancing out of the factors.

On the other hand, the expected results do not hold true for all cases, indicating the intransitiveness of the factors. The table shows that "humanitarianism/allies" has an equal approval level with "humanitarianism/high cost." This leads to the conclusion that a negative factor, "high cost," has the same level *and direction* of influence as a positive factor, "aid to allies." It may be, as suggested in the text, that a factor such as humanitarianism can render inoperative positive or negative factors accompanying it.

Notes

Chapter 1

1. Henry Hazlitt, *Will Dollars Save the World?* (New York: Appleton-Century, 1961).
2. Charles Burton Marshall, "Strategy and Purpose in United States Foreign Policy," in Robert A. Goldwin (ed.), *Beyond the Cold War* (Chicago: Rand McNally, 1965), p. 9.
3. A history of these early technical assistance projects may be found in Merle Curti and Kendall Birr, *Prelude to Point Four* (Madison: The University of Wisconsin Press, 1954).
4. For the story of the Marshall Plan and the politics surrounding its approval, see Joseph M. Jones, *The Fifteen Weeks* (New York: Viking, 1955); and Harry Bayard Price, *The Marshall Plan and Its Meaning* (Ithaca, N.Y.: Cornell University Press, 1955).
5. The reader may also wish to consult four useful sources on the development of foreign aid policy. The first, a guide to foreign policy analysis combined with a collection of the major documents of foreign aid policy, is David A. Baldwin, *Foreign Aid and American Foreign Policy* (New York: Praeger, 1966). The second, by the same author, is an astute analysis of postwar American policy: David A. Baldwin, *Economic Development and American Foreign Policy: 1943–1963* (Chicago: University of Chicago Press, 1966). The third is "The Evolution of Foreign Aid: 1945–1964," in *Congress and the*

Nation (Washington, D.C.: Congressional Quarterly, Inc., 1965), pp. 160–186. The fourth traces interrelationships between domestic and international politics. John D. Montgomery, *The Politics of Foreign Aid* (New York: Praeger, 1962).

6. In the use of terminology and much of the organization of what follows, the studies of public opinion by Gabriel Almond have been extremely influential. See especially his modern classic, *The American People and Foreign Policy* (New York: Praeger, 1960).

Chapter 2

1. This basic doctrine of social psychology has been repeated within the context of political science by V. O. Key, *Public Opinion* (New York: Knopf, 1961), pp. 7, 237. Also see Almond, *op. cit.*, p. 10.

2. It is fashionable to denigrate public opinions as naive since they are based on simplistic analogies. But officials themselves seem to rely on rather elementary analogies at times. Charles Wilson, Dwight Eisenhower's Secretary of Defense, opposed the President's plan to increase economic relations with Communist countries because, he said, "I don't like to sell firearms to the Indians." (Sherman Adams, *Firsthand Report* [New York: Popular Library, 1962], p. 74.)

3. For a historian's well-balanced critique of generalizations about national opinions, see David M. Potter, *People of Plenty* (Chicago: University of Chicago Press, 1954), especially pp. 41–42. Also see Key, *op. cit.*, pp. 49–50.

4. Frank R. Klingberg, "The Historical Alternation of Moods in American Foreign Policy," *World Politics*, IV (January 1952), 239–273.

5. American Institute of Public Opinion [hereinafter cited as AIPO], *Public Opinion News Service* (September 15, 1957); AIPO poll #610 (February 1959); AIPO poll #612 (March 1959); AIPO poll #616 (July 1959); AIPO poll #618 (September 1959); AIPO poll #635 (September 1960).

6. See, for example, Key, *op. cit.*, pp. 106–107.

7. National Opinion Research Center, *American Programs of Foreign Aid* (February 1957), processed, pp. 2, 4 [hereinafter cited as NORC].

8. *Ibid.*, pp. 16, 21.

9. *Ibid.*, p. 2. Italics added.

10. AIPO poll #617 (August 1959).

11. *Ibid.*, (March 1966).

12. William Appleman Williams, *The Tragedy of American Diplomacy* (Cleveland: The World Publishing Co., 1959), p. 24.

13. AIPO poll (March 1966). The same types of aid received 85 per cent approval in an earlier survey (NORC, p. 16).
14. Willard L. Thorp in Grayson Kirk, *et al., The Changing Environment of International Relations* (Washington, D.C.: The Brookings Institution, 1956), p. 118.
15. See, for example, AIPO poll #640 (January 1961).
16. *Meet the Press,* 5 (December 24, 1961), 10.
17. Warren Frederick Ilchman, *Professional Diplomacy In the United States 1779–1939* (Chicago: University of Chicago Press, 1961), p. 35. Ilchman also quotes an apt comment dating from 1880 which bears upon present attitudes: "Americans have not yet quite got over the idea that they are competent to undertake at the shortest possible notice any position calling forth human skill, wit, and activity, no matter how incongruous for such a position a man's antecedents and previous surroundings may have been." (*Ibid.,* p. 59).
18. Geoffrey Gorer, *The American People* (New York: Norton, 1948), p. 224.
19. NORC, pp. 7–8.
20. Hans J. Morgenthau, *The Purpose of American Politics* (New York: Knopf, 1960), p. 190.
21. Many others have commented in similar fashion. See, for example, *ibid.;* William G. Carleton, "Brain-Trusters of American Foreign Policy," *World Politics,* VII (July 1955), 627–639; Norman B. Hannah, "The American People–Foreign Policy and the Foreign Service," *Foreign Service Journal,* 33 (March 1956), 20–21, 42–45, 56; and Potter, *op. cit.,* pp. 112, 138. Daniel Boorstin has called the most active believers in the American mission "singulists." *America and the Image of Europe* (New York: Meridian Books, 1960), pp. 123–127. The present discussion differs from Boorstin in arguing that "singulism" not only may lead to hostility to foreign aid, but may also—up to a point—provide the basis for foreign aid support.
22. NORC, p. 7.
23. *Ibid.,* p. 18.
24. For a survey of such public discussion see Department of State, *American Opinion Report* (January 16, 1962).
25. Gorer, *op. cit.,* p. 225.
26. See, for example, Department of State, *American Opinion Report* (August 1965).
27. Gorer, *op. cit.,* pp. 230–231. See also Potter, *op. cit.,* pp. 111–112; Key, *op. cit.,* pp. 213–214; Almond, *op. cit.,* pp. 54–68.
28. NORC, pp. 5–6.
29. *Ibid.,* pp. 12–13. But see below for some complications in the support of military assistance.
30. NORC, p. 19; and *Minnesota Poll on Foreign Aid* (no place

of publication: November 17, 1961, processed). For a summary of more general public dissatisfaction with aid to neutrals, see Department of State, *American Opinion Report* (May–July 1961), and *ibid.* (December 1964).

31. Surveys of public reaction, such as those in the Department of State's *American Opinion Report,* illustrate this point. These conclusions are, of course, the author's, not those of the Report.

32. Alexis de Tocqueville, *Democracy in America* (New York: Vintage Books, 1958), vol. I, p. 237.

33. NORC, p. 16.

34. *Ibid.*, p. 9.

35. *Ibid.*, p. 12.

36. *Ibid.*, p. 15.

37. *Ibid.*, p. 12.

38. AIPO poll (March 1966).

39. Key, *op. cit.*, pp. 213–214. On this general trait in the American character, see Richard Hofstadter, *Anti-Intellectualism in American Life* (New York: Vintage Books, 1966).

40. Department of State, *American Opinion Report* (July 3, 1962).

41. Robert E. Asher, "The Economics of U.S. Foreign Policy," *Department of State Bulletin* [hereinafter abbreviated as DSB], XXIX (July 5, 1953), 3. George Kennan is one of the best known critics of this tendency of American foreign policy. See his *American Diplomacy 1900–1950* (New York: Mentor, 1952), especially pp. 66–67.

42. NORC, pp. 5–6, 17.

43. On this point see Jahangir Amuzegar, "Point Four: Performance and Prospect," *Political Science Quarterly,* LXXIII (December 1958), 481–546; and Sayre P. Schatz, "The American Approach to Foreign Aid and the Thesis of Low Absorptive Capacity," *The Quarterly Review of Economics and Business,* 1 (November 1961), 55–62.

44. NORC, p. 3. Some indication of the American feeling of competence in economic policy can be seen from the fact that on these two questions, touching on a subject which has turned out to be extremely complex, the number of respondents who admitted to no knowledge or opinion was only 5 and 15 per cent, respectively.

45. *Ibid.*, p. 8.

46. For a summary of such arguments see Department of State, *American Opinion Report* (May–July 1961).

47. AIPO poll #609 (January 1959).

48. NORC, p. 18.

49. "America's Mood," *Look* (June 29, 1965).

50. Cited in Key, *op. cit.*, p. 430. For more recent public expressions of opposition to the financial aspect of aid see *ibid.*, pp. 35, 161.

51. AIPO poll #622 (December 1959).
52. AIPO poll (March 1966).
53. See AIPO poll #596 (March 1958); *ibid.*, #667 (February 1963); and *Newsweek* (August 26, 1963), p. 27. Gallup has asked about general approval of foreign aid four times since 1958, with an average favorable response of 55 per cent.
54. NORC, p. 19.
55. Department of State, *American Opinion Report* (January 16, 1962).
56. NORC, pp. 2–3.
57. Key, *op. cit.*, p. 166.
58. *Ibid.*, pp. 212–214.

Chapter 3

1. Thomas Bailey, *The Man In The Street* (New York: Macmillan, 1948).
2. *Ibid.*, and Samuel Lubell, *The Future of American Politics* (New York: Doubleday, 1956).
3. Key, *op. cit.*, p. 107.
4. AIPO poll #640 (January 1961).
5. See Charles O. Lerche, Jr., "Southern Congressmen and the 'New Isolationism,'" *Political Science Quarterly*, LXXV (September 1960), 321–327.
6. Max Lerner, *America As a Civilization* (New York: Simon and Schuster, 1957), p. 892.
7. Lerche, *loc. cit.*
8. AIPO poll #596 (March 1958).
9. Data pointing toward this conclusion may be found in the poll on the Peace Corps (AIPO poll #640, January 1961), in which the South's approval level was only 3 percentage points below the national average of 71 per cent. Also see the discussion in Lerche, *The Uncertain South* (Chicago: Quadrangle Books, 1964), esp. pp. 247–291.
10. AIPO poll #609 (January 1959).
11. This is only the briefest discussion of a complex subject. The interested reader is referred to the massive analysis of the South and American foreign policy, Alfred Hero, *The Southerner and World Affairs* (Baton Rouge: Louisiana State University Press, 1965).
12. AIPO poll #597 (March 1958). This point will be more fully explored in Chapter 4.
13. These figures are from AIPO poll #596 (March 1958). As Key notes, differences in attitude associated with occupation on economic policy are easily explicable on the basis of perceived self-interest. The reason for clearly established differ-

ences among these groups on foreign policy questions is not so evident. Key, *op. cit.,* pp. 130–131.

14. AIPO poll #576 (December 1956). Also see Bruce M. Russett, "Demography, Salience, and Isolationist Behavior," *Public Opinion Quarterly,* XXIV (Winter 1960), 658–664, for other supporting evidence on the distribution of intensities.

15. Key, *op. cit.,* pp. 187, 190–191, 195–197.

16. AIPO poll #609 (January 1959).

17. *Congressional Record* (May 2, 1960), p. 9027.

18. See, for example, Stanley Kelley, Jr., "The Presidential Campaign," in Paul T. David (ed.), *The Presidential Election and Transition, 1960–1961* (Washington, D.C.: The Brookings Institution, 1961), pp. 66–67. The candidates' speeches were compiled in the Senate Committee on Interstate and Foreign Commerce, *Freedom of Communications:* Parts I and II, 87th Congress, 1st Session. [Cited hereinafter as *Freedom of Communications.*]

19. Kelley, *op. cit.,* p. 66.

20. This analysis closely follows Donald E. Stokes, "Spatial Models of Party Competition," *American Political Science Review,* LVII (June 1963), 368–377.

21. *Freedom of Communications,* Part II, p. 460.

22. *Ibid.,* pp. 85–86.

23. *Ibid.,* p. 218.

24. Kelley, *op. cit.,* pp. 66–69.

25. For summaries of these debates, see *ibid.,* pp. 75–77, 81–83.

26. *Freedom of Communications,* Part I, p. 419.

27. *Ibid.,* p. 343.

28. *Ibid.,* pp. 381, 489, 581.

29. *Freedom of Communications,* Part II, p. 461.

30. *Ibid.,* p. 258.

31. *Ibid.,* p. 462.

32. *Freedom of Communications,* Part I, p. 865.

33. *Freedom of Communications,* Part II, p. 1061. Nixon's heavy emphasis on the "draft evasion" theme suggests that he was reacting to the advance text of Kennedy's speech, in which the relevant passage ran, "as an alternative to peacetime selective service," instead of the more ambiguous phrase quoted above, which Kennedy actually used. For the advance text see *Freedom of Communications,* Part I, p. 1237.

34. John M. Hightower, in Paul T. David, *op. cit.,* p. 177.

35. This is hardly surprising, since all candidates use information about the electorate gathered and analyzed by professional or academic pollsters. One of the most sophisticated of these operations was conducted for Kennedy in 1960. For a description, see Ithiel de Sola Pool, Robert P. Abelson, and Samuel

Popkin, *Candidates, Issues, and Strategies* (Cambridge, Mass.: The MIT Press, 1965).

36. *Ibid.*, pp. 177–179.
37. George Belknap and Angus Campbell, "Political Party Identification and Attitudes toward Foreign Policy," *Public Opinion Quarterly*, 15 (Winter 1952), 618.
38. *Ibid.*, p. 619.
39. Bernard Berleson *et al.*, *Voting* (Chicago: The University of Chicago Press, 1954), p. 198.
40. Angus Campbell *et al.*, *The American Voter* (New York: Wiley, 1960), p. 182.
41. *Ibid.*
42. Some of those associations are concisely related in Lerner, *op. cit.*, pp. 889–891.
43. This story is recounted in Richard Hofstadter, *The American Political Tradition* (New York: Vintage Books, 1960), pp. 283–314. The quotation is found on p. 289.
44. Harry S Truman, *Year of Decisions* (New York: Doubleday, 1955), p. 472.
45. See Key, *op. cit.*; and Seymour Martin Lipset, *Political Man* (New York: Doubleday, 1960).
46. Key, *op. cit.*, p. 157.
47. AIPO polls #609 (January 1959) and #640 (January 1961).
48. The three occupational groups which alone gave over 60 per cent support to foreign aid on the general question supported the Peace Corps by an average of 73 per cent. The remainder of the population, averaging 47 per cent on foreign aid in general, supported the Peace Corps by an average of 69 per cent.
49. *Meet the Press*, 5 (December 24, 1961), 3–4.
50. Estimate based on *Payment to U.S. Firms* (Washington, D.C.: International Cooperative Administration, May 1961).
51. *Congressional Quarterly*, XIX (August 4, 1961), 1353–1357.
52. This category is of occasional interest, as will be seen in the discussion of the legislature and the executive.
53. A high level of education, the one variable clearly associated with support for foreign aid, is rarely the core of politically meaningful organizations.
54. Senate Foreign Relations Committee, *International Development and Security. Hearings on S. 1983*, 87th Congress, 1st Session, p. 952.
55. Nearly all of the first two sets of groups share this characteristic to some extent. The proponents of aid are sufficiently optimistic to think American values and institutions can be transmitted abroad. The opponents are so pessimistic as to believe that such things have not been and cannot be transmitted.

56. These arguments are found in many places. The foregoing generalizations are based on public literature, statements, and interviews with pressure group representatives. The most easily accessible collections of a wide variety of pressure-group opinions are found in the published annual testimony of House and Senate Hearings. See, for example, Senate Foreign Relations Committee, *op. cit.*, pp. 887–1221; and Senate Appropriations Committee, *Foreign Assistance and Related Agencies Appropriations for 1962*, 87th Congress, 1st Session, pp. 601–693.
57. The Congressman can occasionally be seen searching for general cues to which to react. See Senate Foreign Relations Committee, *op. cit.*, pp. 1008–1009.
58. The anti-aid CFAC claimed with satisfaction that it had received only five unfavorable (that is, pro-aid) letters in four years.
59. See Key, *op. cit.*, pp. 515–517; and Bernard C. Cohen, *The Political Process and Foreign Policy* (Princeton, N.J.: Princeton University Press, 1957), pp. 101, 103.
60. Senate Foreign Relations Committee, *op. cit.*, pp. 952–953.

Chapter 4

1. *Congressional Quarterly*, XIX (January 6, 1961), 15. Available figures do not permit a more precise statement since some members list more than one occupation. In the 87th Congress, 63 per cent of the Senate and 56 per cent of the House listed the occupation of lawyer; corresponding figures in the Senate and House for other professions were business or banking: 31 per cent and 31 per cent; teaching: 14 per cent and 9 per cent; medicine or engineering: 3 per cent and 2 per cent.
2. AIPO poll #596 (March 1958).
3. This figure was derived from all roll call votes during the 86th and 87th Congresses on foreign aid authorizations and appropriations, American participation in international aid and lending activities, "Food for Peace" provisions of Public Law 480, the Peace Corps, and attempts to encourage private investment in underdeveloped nations. There were 96 such votes in the Senate and 32 in the House of Representatives. Every position supporting higher dollar figures or opposing administrative restrictions was counted as a "pro-aid" position. Scores were computed on the basis of votes, pairs, and announced positions as reported by the *Congressional Quarterly*. The figure is only an approximation; a weighted average was determined on the basis of the number of Congressmen in each decile of support from 0 per cent to 100 per cent. These

figures are used later in the chapter in discussing various aspects of support for foreign aid.

The time period used, 1959–1962, is interesting because it is the most recent period in which the party in the White House changed and the majority in Congress remained the same. As we shall observe below, party affiliation of Congressmen and the President is quite important.

4. DSB, LIII (July 12, 1965), 66–70.
5. For the text of the reply see *Congressional Record* (July 28, 1959), p. 14478.
6. See, for example, *ibid.* (August 16, 1961), p. 16048.
7. *The New York Times* (January 15, 1964).
8. We do not have, however, what may be highly important information: How and to what extent foreign aid has been used as an election issue by opposing congressional candidates.
9. It should be recalled that the procedures of the two houses account for at least part of the difference in the distribution of scores, which are based on roll-call votes.
10. Richard E. Neustadt, *Presidential Power* (New York: Wiley, 1960), pp. 3 and 191.
11. This repetition has been described in various ways—"ritual," "battle," "dialogue." In a recent book (*Witness for Aid* [Boston: Houghton Mifflin, 1964]), AID Deputy Administrator Frank Coffin calls this process a "minuet." Others have suggested that because of the appropriation process in particular, this annual dance might better be labeled the "Twist."
12. Members of both authorizing and appropriating committees vote in approximately the same fashion on foreign aid whether they are voting for their own committee's bill or a bill from another committee.
13. *Congressional Record* (June 17, 1960), p. 13104.
14. *Ibid.*
15. Elizabeth Drew, "Mr. Passman Meets His Match," *The Reporter*, 31 (November 19, 1964), 40-43.
16. For a description of this by Congressman Walter Judd, see *Congressional Record* (July 28, 1959), p. 14492.
17. See Congressman Mahon's views, above.
18. The foregoing may be considered a partial illustration, with some generic differences, of Aaron Wildavsky's study of the politics of budgeting, *The Politics of the Budgetary Process* (Boston: Little, Brown, 1964).
19. The argument for possible relationships between opinion and voting must be made on the basis of inspection of the figures. The deviations of the Rocky Mountain and East Central Regions produce low statistical scores of correlation. Spearman's rank-order correlation is .4 for both the House and the Senate. The complex relationships between constituent opinion and

congressional voting is just beginning to receive intensive analysis. See Warren E. Miller and Donald E. Stokes, "Constituency Influence in Congress," *American Political Science Review*, LVII (March 1963), 45–56; and Charles F. Cnudde and Donald J. McCrone, "The Linkage Between Constituency Attitudes and Congressional Voting Behavior: A Causal Model," *ibid.*, LX (March 1966), 66–72. For a masterful analysis of the subtle interactions between Congress and its political environment, see Raymond A. Bauer, Ithiel de Sola Pool, and Lewis Anthony Dexter, *American Business and Public Policy* (New York: Atherton Press, 1963).

20. The use of alleged public pressure to justify legislative decisions often results in statements of rather complex political philosophy. Consider, for example, the following pronouncement in which adhering to voters' wishes is justified by an intriguing mixture of principle and electoral expediency: "when it comes to a matter of principle I . . . listen to the folks who, in my judgment, know best. Maybe I am influenced by the fact that we are re-elected by the home folk. I follow them always, unless they want something that I think is injurious to the welfare of the people as a whole." *Congressional Record* (August 18, 1961) p. 16282.

21. Key, *op. cit.*, p. 418.

22. *Ibid.*, p. 499. On this same point see Dahl, *Congress and Foreign Policy* (New York: Harcourt, Brace & World, 1950), p. 37.

23. *Congressional Record* (April 20, 1960), p. 8391. In at least one recent campaign a Mississippi Congressman who had supported foreign aid was defeated by an opponent who relied upon antagonism to foreign aid, including the Peace Corps, almost as much as that hardy Southern perennial, civil rights. See Frank Smith, *Congressman From Mississippi* (New York: Pantheon Books, 1964).

24. *The New York Times* (November 9, 1963), p. 11.

25. See Miller and Stokes, *op. cit.*, pp. 45–46, which attempts to measure in rigorous fashion the relative influences of constituency, party, and executive branch on legislative behavior. The tentative conclusions of Miller and Stokes are less directly concerned with the question of foreign aid, but they are consistent with the discussion of this study.

26. H. B. Westerfield, *Foreign Policy and Party Politics* (New Haven: Yale University Press, 1955), pp. 4–5. Also see Campbell, *op cit.*, p. 182.

27. Lewis Anthony Dexter, *Congress and the People They Listen To* (Cambridge, Mass.: Center for International Studies, Massachusetts Institute of Technology, 1955), mimeographed,

I, 2–3; on this same point see also Dahl, *op. cit.*, pp. 15, 134–135.

28. *Congressional Record* (April 3, 1962), p. 5826.
29. *Ibid.* (September 14, 1961), p. 19508.
30. *Ibid.* (April 3, 1962), p. 5826.
31. *Ibid.* (September 14, 1961), p. 19507.
32. *Ibid.* (April 3, 1962), p. 5831.
33. These totals lump together authorization and appropriation bill amendments, since preliminary analysis showed no significant differences between the two.
34. These included technical questions such as specifying how certain Presidential reports on foreign aid should be published. They also included such peripheral questions as the means of selecting delegates to the Interparliamentary Union and the assurance that nothing in the aid bill would prohibit other funds from being spent on the New York World's Fair.
35. *Congressional Record* (August 16, 1961), p. 15979.
36. *Ibid.* (July 7, 1959), p. 12777.
37. *Ibid.* (June 17, 1959), p. 11125.
38. *Ibid.*, p. 11122.
39. Dahl, *op. cit.*, p. 82.
40. *Congressional Record* (July 2, 1959), p. 12564.
41. United States Congress, House, Committee on Foreign Relations, *Report on the Mutual Security Program* (Washington: Government Printing Office, 1959), p. 51.
42. Roger Davidson *et al.*, *Congress in Crisis* (Belmont, California: Wadsworth Publishing Company, 1966).
43. *Congressional Record* (June 16, 1959), p. 10960.
44. The source of much of this evidence of wrong-doing cited by aid opponents has been the Government Operations Subcommittee on Foreign Operations and Monetary Affairs. It is interesting to note that four of the five members of the committee, including Chairman Porter Hardy, accumulated aid-support scores of 70 per cent or more, well in excess of the average.
45. *Congressional Record* (July 2, 1959), p. 12561.
46. *Ibid.* (August 15, 1961), pp. 15851–15852.

Chapter 5

1. Neustadt, *op. cit.*, p. 5.
2. DSB, XXXVIII (May 26, 1958), 881.
3. DSB, XLIX (October 7, 1963), 597–598.
4. DSB, XX (February 6, 1949), 155; also DSB, XXI (August 29, 1949), 305–306.
5. DSB, XXVI (April 21, 1952), 612.
6. DSB, (March 17, 1952), 407.
7. DSB, XXVIII (February 23, 1953), 315.

8. DSB, XXXIII (December 19, 1955), 1006.

9. DSB, XLI (September 14, 1959), 376.

10. DSB, XXII (April 10, 1950), 552; and DSB, XXIII (July 10, 1950), 66.

11. DSB, XXIII (July 10, 1950), 66.

12. DSB, XLI (September 14, 1959), 376.

13. DSB, XLIV (June 26, 1961), 1006.

14. See DSB, XXXIX (October 27, 1958), 656–657.

15. See, for example, Harold Stassen, "The Case for Private Investment Abroad," *Foreign Affairs*, 32 (April 1954), 402–415; DSB, XXIV (June 18, 1956), 1006–1013; and DSB, XXVII (October 6, 1952), 538–541.

16. See Andrew Schonfield, *The Attack on World Poverty* (New York: Random House, 1960), pp. 26–29; and William Adams Brown, Jr., and Redvers Opie, *American Foreign Assistance* (Washington, D.C.: The Brookings Institution, 1953), p. 419.

17. DSB, XXXV (July 23, 1956), 136–137.

18. DSB, XX (March 27, 1949), 374; and DSB, XXXIX (December 15, 1958), 969.

19. DSB, XXX (January 11, 1954), 51.

20. DSB, XXXVIII (February 24, 1958), 296.

21. DSB, XXIV (June 18, 1956), 1008.

22. Some of the problems connected with private capital were indicated by a report early in the Kennedy Administration showing that in 1960 American investors took out of the underdeveloped countries $900,000,000 more than they put in. DSB, XLV (December 25, 1961), 1051.

23. *The Mutual Security Program for Fiscal Year 1952* (Washington: Government Printing Office, 1951), p. 25; *The Mutual Security Program for Fiscal Year 1953* (Washington: Government Printing Office, 1952), p. 25; and DSB, XXI (September 26, 1949), 465.

24. This discussion generally excludes multilateral activities, since bilateral policies have been the source of the chief political debate. American policies in the international field have generally paralleled those in the national. The chief source of multilateral capital has been the International Bank for Reconstruction and Development which, like the EXIM Bank, works through private investors to make loans on profitable enterprises. It is largely influenced by the United States because of its voting procedures and its sources of capital. The expansion of international aid activities in the late 1950s was through the IBRD rather than the United Nations, where American influence (and Western domination) of policies could have been lost to the underdeveloped countries.

25. DSB, XXIX (October 27, 1958), 647; and DSB, XXXIV (January 30, 1956), 161.

26. DSB, XXXIX (October 13, 1958), 561. Also see The Brookings Institution, *Governmental Mechanism for the Conduct of United States Foreign Relations* (Washington, D.C.: The Brookings Institution, 1949), p. 30.

27. See DSB, XXXVIII (January 27, 1958), 141.

28. One can almost see a law of policy innovation: the newer the policies, the more ancient the symbols which are invoked on their behalf. The Peace Corps has been cast in the mold of Jeffersonian idealism. National planning and government-induced income redistribution have been defended with Adam Smith's doctrines on the need for government to create the framework within which a modern economy can develop. DSB, XLIX (September 16, 1963), 424.

29. DSB, XLI (November 2, 1959), 636.

30. *Ibid.*, 636–637 (italics in original).

31. *Ibid.*, 637.

32. DSB, XXIX (October 19, 1953), 516.

33. DSB, XLI (November 2, 1959), 637.

34. DSB, XLIV (March 27, 1961), 456.

35. See DSB, XXXVIII (February 10, 1958), 208–209.

36. Clearly stated in DSB, XXXIV (June 18, 1956), 1013.

37. *Ibid.*, 1009–1010.

38. DSB, XXXIX (October 27, 1958), 656.

39. *Ibid.*, XLII (June 6, 1960), 930.

40. *Foreign Aspects of U.S. National Security. Conference Report and Proceedings* (Washington, D.C.: Committee for International Economic Growth, April 1958), p. 17.

41. DSB, XLV (September 18, 1961), 492.

42. *Ibid.* (November 20, 1961), 839–840.

43. DSB, XXII (June 26, 1950), 1060.

44. DSB, XLIII (December 5, 1960), 856–857; and DSB, XLIV (March 6, 1961), 378.

45. DSB, XLIX (July 1, 1963), 21.

46. DSB, XLV (September 18, 1961), 482; DSB, XLV (December 11, 1961), 984–986; DSB, L (March 23, 1964), 436.

47. Teodoro Moscoso, "The Alliance for Progress" (Washington: Agency for International Development, n.d.). For a later example see "Aid Figures Illustrate U.S. Help to Alliance," AID press release (March 28, 1966).

48. See H. Schuyler Foster, "Does Press Comment Represent Public Opinion?" (May 15, 1953), processed. Mr. Foster is the Director of the Public Opinion Studies Staff in the Department of State.

49. For information on this prohibition see Andrew Eliot Rice, "Building a Constituency for the Foreign Aid Program: The Record of the Eisenhower Years" (Ph.D. dissertation, Syracuse University, 1963), pp. 75–77.

Chapter 6

1. Divergence of this sort has also been discovered elsewhere in American politics. See Herbert McClosky *et al.*, "Issue Conflict and Consensus Among Party Leaders and Followers," *American Political Science Review*, LIV (June 1960), 406–427. For a study of the community of aid supporters and their relationship to the government, James Rosenau, *National Leadership and Foreign Policy* (Princeton, N.J.: Princeton University Press, 1963).
2. James MacGregor Burns, *Deadlock of Democracy* (Englewood Cliffs, N.J.: Prentice-Hall, 1963).
3. This is not to say that anti-aid arguments are of necessity simplistic. There are many sophisticated criticisms of particular aid policies and aid in general. The point is that there are many effective simplistic arguments against foreign aid, but relatively few in favor.
4. It is fascinating to speculate on the extent to which officials actually rely on these values in making policy, and the extent to which they merely explain policy in terms they feel the public will understand and approve. Robert Packenham has suggested that operating officials have less grandiose expectations than public statements would suggest. Robert Packenham, "Political-Development Doctrines in the American Foreign Aid Program," *World Politics*, XVIII (January 1966), 194–235.
5. Jones, *op. cit.*, p. 252.
6. Price, *op. cit.*, pp. 55–56.
7. For commentary on the Clay Committee in particular, see Usha Mahanji, "Kennedy and the Strategy of Aid," *Western Political Quarterly*, XVIII (September 1965), 656–668.
8. See Key, *op. cit.*, p. 214, for relevant data on public attitudes.
9. DSB, XXXII (May 2, 1955), 715–716.
10. For one of many examples, see *Highlights of President Kennedy's New Act for International Development* (Washington: Government Printing Office, 1961), p. 24.
11. *The New York Times* (November 18, 1962).
12. For an excellent account, see Paul Duke, "The Foreign Aid Fiasco," *The Reporter* (January 16, 1964), pp. 20–25; and Mahanji, *op. cit.*
13. Coffin, *op. cit.*, p. 43.
14. See *Cooperative-Democratic Institutions for Economic and Social Development. A Report by the Special Advisory Committee on Cooperatives to the Administrator of the Agency for International Development* (November 1, 1961), processed.
15. Department of State, *American Opinion Report* (January 16, 1962).

16. The general idea of separation for the sake of public appeal became strong enough in 1961 to provoke serious consideration of transforming the Latin American Bureau of AID into an independent "Alliance for Progress Agency."

17. *The New York Times* (September 8, 1963).

18. These results shed additional light on the attempt in Chapter 2 and the Appendix to evaluate the relative strengths of positive and negative values associated with foreign aid. The general success of military aid is consistent with the earlier conclusion that the positive force of assisting allies is stronger than the negative effect of deep involvement. The harsher legislative treatment of DLF and the Contingency Fund is less clearly related to the earlier analysis. It may be partly due to the fact that while these programs are only ambiguously associated with missionary appeals and aid to allies, the DLF clearly implies the negative factors of high cost and deep involvement. The apparently great concern with congressional control (a value not analyzed in public opinion polls) also works to the disadvantage of the DLF and the Contingency Fund.

19. Foreign aid support scores were compiled by the author. Other Presidential support scores have been used as compiled by *Congressional Quarterly*.

20. This does not prevent the Agency from using after-the-fact publicity. See the press release dated June 28, 1962, "Foreign Aid Program Saves 1100 Jobs for Steel Works in Birmingham, Ala." The release was issued from the office of Senator John Sparkman.

21. *U.S. News and World Report*, LII (April 23, 1962), 1.

22. *Payment to U.S. Firms* (Washington, D.C.: International Cooperation Administration, May 1961).

23. For an instructive segment of the debate see *Congressional Record*, Senate (August 11, 1961), p. 15571.

24. *The New York Times* (August 30, 1961).

25. Many of these dogmas have been ably dissected by Professor David Baldwin. See his "The International Bank in Political Perspective," *World Politics*, XVIII (October 1965), 68–81; and *Economic Development and American Foreign Policy: 1943–1963*.

26. Theodore White, *The Making of the President, 1964* (New York: Atheneum, 1965), p. 213.

27. Much of the appeal of Goldwaterism and parallel views of the world may arise from a generalization of this style of thinking. The carrot has not been useful in tempting other nations to move in directions consistent with American goals; perhaps the stick will propel them.

28. See Robert Asher, *Grants, Loans, and Local Currencies* (Washington, D.C.: The Brookings Institution, 1961).
29. DSB, LII (April 5, 1965), 485–486.
30. Louis T. Halle, *The Society of Man* (New York: Harper & Row, n.d.), pp. 21–23.
31. See Harlan Cleveland, Introduction to Robert G. A. Jackson, *The Case for an International Development Authority* (Syracuse, N.Y.: Syracuse University Press, 1959); and Dean Acheson, "The President and the Secretary of State," in Don Price (ed.), *The Secretary of State* (Englewood Cliffs, N.J.: Prentice-Hall, 1960), p. 49.

Bibliography

Books

Acheson, Dean. *A Citizen Looks at Congress*. New York: Harper & Row, 1957.

Adams, Sherman. *Firsthand Report*. New York: Popular Library, 1962.

Almond, Gabriel. *The American People and Foreign Policy*. New York: Praeger, 1960.

——. "Introductory: Comparative Study of Foreign Policy," in Roy Macridis, ed., *Foreign Policy in World Politics*. Englewood Cliffs, N.J.: Prentice-Hall, 1958.

Andrews, Stanley. *The Farmer's Dilemma*. Washington, D.C.: Public Affairs Press, 1961.

Asher, Robert E. *Grants, Loans, and Local Currencies*. Washington, D.C.: The Brookings Institution, 1961.

Bailey, Thomas. *The Man In the Street*. New York: Macmillan, 1948.

Baldwin, David A. *Economic Development and American Foreign Policy: 1943-1963*. Chicago: The University of Chicago Press, 1966.

——. *Foreign Aid and American Foreign Policy*. New York: Praeger, 1966.

Banfield, Edward C. "American Foreign Aid Doctrines," in Carl J. Friedrich and Seymour Harris, eds., *Public Policy*, Volume XI. Cambridge, Mass.: Graduate School of Public Administration, 1961.

Bauer, Raymond A., Ithiel de Sola Pool, and Lewis Anthony Dexter. *American Business and Public Policy*. New York: Atherton Press, 1963.

Beloff, Max. *Foreign Policy and the Democratic Process*. Baltimore: The Johns Hopkins Press, 1955.

Benham, Frederic. *Economic Aid to Underdeveloped Countries*. London: Oxford University Press, 1961.

Berelson, Bernard, *et al. Voting*. Chicago: The University of Chicago Press, 1954.

Black, Eugene R. *The Diplomacy of Economic Development and Other Papers*. New York: Atheneum, 1963.

Boorstin, Daniel. *America and the Image of Europe*. New York: Meridian Books, 1960.

Broekmeijer, M. W. J. M. *Developing Countries and N.A.T.O.* Leyden: A. W. Sythoff, 1963.

The Brookings Institution. *Governmental Mechanism for the Conduct of United States Foreign Relations*. Washington, D.C.: The Brookings Institution, 1949.

Brown, William Adams, Jr., and Redvers Opie. *American Foreign Assistance*. Washington, D.C.: The Brookings Institution, 1953.

Buehrig, Edward H. *Woodrow Wilson and the Balance of Power*. Bloomington: Indiana University Press, 1955.

Burns, James MacGregor. *Deadlock of Democracy*. Englewood Cliffs, N.J.: Prentice-Hall, 1963.

Campbell, Angus, *et al. The American Voter*. New York: Wiley, 1960.

——. *The Voter Decides*. New York: Harper & Row, 1954.

Carroll, Holbert N. *The House of Representatives and Foreign Affairs*. Pittsburgh: University of Pittsburgh Press, 1958.

Cheever, Daniel S., and H. Field Haviland, Jr. *American Foreign Policy and the Separation of Powers*. Cambridge: Harvard University Press, 1952.

Childs, Harwood. *An Introduction to Public Opinion*. New York: Wiley, 1940.

Coffin, Frank. *Witness for Aid*. Boston: Houghton Mifflin, 1964.

Cohen, Bernard C. "American Foreign Policy," in Roy Macridis, ed., *Foreign Policy in World Politics*. Englewood Cliffs, N.J.: Prentice-Hall, 1958.

——. *The Political Process and Foreign Policy*. Princeton, N.J.: Princeton University Press, 1957.

Colegrove, Kenneth. *The American Senate and World Peace*. New York: The Vanguard Press, 1944.

Congress and the Nation. Washington, D.C.: Congressional Quarterly, Inc., 1965.

Corwin, Edward S. *The President's Control of Foreign Relations*. Princeton, N.J.: Princeton University Press, 1917.

Cox, Oliver C. *Capitalism and American Leadership*. New York: Philosophical Library, 1962.

Crabb, Cecil V. *Bipartisan Foreign Policy. Myth or Reality?* New York: Harper & Row, 1957.

Curti, Merle, and Kendall Birr. *Prelude to Point Four*. Madison: The University of Wisconsin Press, 1954.

Dahl, Robert. *Congress and Foreign Policy*. New York: Harcourt, Brace and World, 1950.

————. *A Preface to Democratic Theory*. Chicago: The University of Chicago Press, 1956.

Davidson, Roger, David Kovenock, and Michael O'Leary. *Congress in Crisis*. Belmont, Calif.: Wadsworth Publishing Company, 1966.

de Sola Pool, Ithiel, Robert P. Abelson, and Samuel Popkin. *Candidates, Issues, and Strategies*. Cambridge, Mass.: The MIT Press, 1965.

de Tocqueville, Alexis. *Democracy in America*. Two volumes. New York: Vintage Books, 1945.

Downs, Anthony. *An Economic Theory of Democracy*. New York: Harper & Row, 1957.

Easton, David. *The Political System*. New York: Knopf, 1953.

Elder, Robert Ellsworth. *The Policy Machine*. Syracuse, N.Y.: Syracuse University Press, 1960.

Farnsworth, David Nelson. *The Senate Committee on Foreign Relations*. Illinois Studies in the Social Sciences, Volume 49. Urbana, Ill.: The University of Illinois Press, 1961.

Foreign Aspects of U.S. National Security. Conference Report and Proceedings. Washington, D.C.: Committee for International Economic Growth, April 1958.

Geiger, Theodore. *The Premium Gold Controversy in the International Monetary Fund*. University, Ala.: University of Alabama Press, 1961.

Gideonse, Harry D. *The Economic Foreign Policy of the United States*. Cairo: National Bank of Egypt, 1953.

Gorer, Geoffrey. *The American People. A Study in National Character*. New York: Norton, 1948.

Halle, Louis T. *The Society of Man*. New York: Harper & Row, 1965.

Hazlitt, Henry. *Will Dollars Save the World?* New York: Appleton-Century-Crofts, 1947.

Hero, Alfred. *The Southerner and World Affairs*. Baton Rouge, La.: Louisiana State University Press, 1965.

Hightower, John M. "The Impact on Foreign Relations," in Paul T. David, ed., *The Presidential Election and Transition 1960-1961*. Washington, D.C.: The Brookings Institution, 1961.

161

Bibliography

Hirschman, Albert O. *The Strategy of Economic Development.* New Haven: Yale University Press, 1958.

Hofstadter, Richard. *The American Political Tradition.* New York: Vintage Books, 1960.

———. *Anti-Intellectualism in American Life.* New York: Vintage Books, 1966.

Ilchman, Warren Frederick. *Professional Diplomacy in the United States 1779-1939.* Chicago: The University of Chicago Press, 1961.

Jackson, Sir Robert G. A. *The Case for an International Development Authority.* Syracuse, N.Y.: Syracuse University Press, 1959.

Jewell, Malcolm E. *Senatorial Politics and Foreign Policy.* Lexington: University of Kentucky Press, 1962.

Jones, Joseph M. *The Fifteen Weeks.* New York: The Viking Press, 1955.

Jordan, Amos A. *Foreign Aid and the Defense of Southeast Asia.* New York: Praeger, 1962.

Kelley, Stanley, Jr. "The Presidential Campaign," in Paul T. David, ed., *The Presidential Election and Transition 1960–1961.* Washington, D.C.: The Brookings Institution, 1961.

Kennan, George F. *American Diplomacy 1900–1950.* New York: Mentor, 1952.

Key, V. O. *Politics, Parties, and Pressure Groups.* New York: Crowell, 1960.

———. *Public Opinion and American Democracy.* New York: Knopf, 1961.

Lerche, Charles O., Jr. *The Uncertain South.* Chicago: Quadrangle Books, 1964.

Lerner, Max. *America As a Civilization.* New York: Simon and Schuster, 1957.

Lipset, Seymour Martin. *Political Man.* New York: Doubleday, 1960.

Liska, George. *The New Statecraft.* Chicago: The University of Chicago Press, 1960.

Lubell, Samuel. *The Future of American Politics.* New York: Doubleday, 1956.

Markel, Lester, *et al. Public Opinion and Foreign Policy.* New York: Harper & Row, 1949.

Marshall, Charles Burton. "Strategy and Purpose in United States Foreign Policy," in Robert A. Goldwin, ed., *Beyond the Cold War.* Chicago: Rand McNally, 1965.

Mikesell, Raymond. *United States Economic Policy and International Relations.* New York: McGraw-Hill, 1952.

Montgomery, John D. *The Politics of Foreign Aid.* New York: Praeger, 1962.

Morgenthau, Hans J. *Dilemmas of Politics*. Chicago: The University of Chicago Press, 1958.

————. *The Purpose of American Politics*. New York: Knopf, 1960.

Myrdal, Gunnar. *Rich Lands and Poor*. New York: Harper & Row, 1957.

Neustadt, Richard E. *Presidential Power*. New York: Wiley, 1960.

Potter, David M. *People of Plenty*. Chicago: The University of Chicago Press, 1954.

Price, Don K., ed. *The Secretary of State*. Englewood Cliffs, N.J.: Prentice-Hall, 1960.

Price, Harry Bayard. *The Marshall Plan and Its Meaning*. Ithaca, N.Y.: Cornell University Press, 1955.

Riesman, David. *Abundance for What?* Garden City, N.Y.: Doubleday, 1964.

Robinson, James A. *Congress and Foreign Policy-Making*. Homewood, Illinois: Dorsey Press, 1962.

Rosenau, James N. *National Leadership and Foreign Policy*. Princeton, N.J.: Princeton University Press, 1963.

————. *Public Opinion and Foreign Policy*. New York: Random House, 1961.

Schelling, Thomas. *International Economics*. Boston: Allyn and Bacon, 1958.

Schlesinger, James R. *The Political Economy of National Security*. New York: Praeger, 1960.

Schonfield, Andrew. *The Attack on World Poverty*. New York: Random House, 1960.

Smith, Frank. *Congressman From Mississippi*. New York: Pantheon Books, 1964.

Staley, Eugene. *The Future of Underdeveloped Countries*. New York: Praeger, 1961.

Thompson, Kenneth W., and Roy Macridis. "Theories and Problems of Foreign Policy," in Roy Macridis, ed., *Foreign Policy in World Politics*. Englewood Cliffs, N.J.: Prentice-Hall, 1958.

Thorp, Willand L., and Grayson Kirk. *The Changing Environment of International Relations*. Washington, D.C.: The Brookings Institution, 1956.

Truman, David B. *The Governmental Process*. New York: Knopf, 1955.

Truman, Harry S. *Year of Decisions*. Garden City, N.Y.: Doubleday, 1955.

Westerfield, H. Bradford. *Foreign Policy and Party Politics*. New Haven: Yale University Press, 1955.

Westphal, Albert C. F. *The House Committee on Foreign Affairs*. New York: Columbia University Press, 1942.

White, Theodore. *The Making of the President, 1964*. New York: Atheneum, 1965.

Bibliography

Wildavsky, Aaron. *The Politics of the Budgetary Process*. Boston: Little, Brown, 1964.
Wilkinson, Joe R. *Politics and Trade Policy*. Washington, D.C.: Public Affairs Press, 1960.
Williams, William Appleman. *The Tragedy of American Diplomacy*. Cleveland: The World Publishing Company, 1959.
Wolf, Charles, Jr. *Foreign Aid: Theory and Practice in Southern Asia*. Princeton, N.J.: Princeton University Press, 1960.

Articles and Periodicals

Almond, Gabriel. Review of Case, Lynn M. *French Opinion on War and Diplomacy during the Second Empire*. *Public Opinion Quarterly*, XXI (Spring 1957), 215-218.
"America's Mood," *Look*, June 29, 1965.
Amuzegar, Jahangir. "Point Four: Performance and Prospect," *Political Science Quarterly*, LXXIII (December 1958), 481-546.
Baldwin, David. "The International Bank in Political Perspective," *World Politics*, XVIII (October 1965), 68-81.
Beckett, Paul L. "*Ad Astra Per Aspera*: Meditations on the Ecology of Technical Assistance Administration," *The Western Political Quarterly*, XI (September 1958), 437-453.
Belknap, George, and Angus Campbell. "Political Party Identification and Attitudes toward Foreign Policy," *Public Opinion Quarterly*, XV (Winter 1952), 601-623.
Carleton, William G. "Brain Trusters of American Foreign Policy," *World Politics*, VII (July 1955).
Cnudde, Charles F., and Donald J. McCrone. "The Linkage Between Constituency Attitudes and Congressional Voting Behavior: A Causal Model," *American Political Science Review*, LVII (March 1966), 66-72.
Cohen, Bernard. Review of William A. Scott and Stephen B. Withey. *The United States and the United Nations: The Public View, 1945-1955*. *Public Opinion Quarterly*, XXIII (Summer 1959), 297-298.
Cozort, William T. "House Opposition to Foreign Aid Legislation," *Southwest Social Science Quarterly*, 42 (September 1961).
Dahl, Robert A. "The Concept of Power," *Behavioral Science*, 2 (July 1957), 201-215.
Drew, Elizabeth. "Mr. Passman Meets His Match," *The Reporter*, 31 (November 19, 1964), 40-43.
Duke, Paul. "The Foreign Aid Fiasco," *The Reporter* (January 16, 1964), 20-25.
Fenno, Richard F., Jr. "The House Appropriations Committee,"

The American Political Science Review, LVI (June 1962), 310–324.

Glickman, Harvey. "Viewing Public Opinion in Politics: A Common Sense Approach," *Public Opinion Quarterly,* XXIII (Winter 1959), 495–504.

Grassmuck, George L. "Sectional Biases in Congress on Foreign Policy," *The Johns Hopkins University Studies in Historical and Political Science,* LXVIII (1950).

Hannah, Norman B. "The American People—Foreign Policy and the Foreign Service," *Foreign Service Journal,* 33 (March 1956), 20–21, 42–45, 56.

Haviland, H. Field, Jr. "Foreign Aid and the Policy Process: 1957," *The American Political Science Review,* LII (September 1958), 689–724.

Hilsman, Roger. "Congressional-Executive Relations and the Foreign Policy Consensus," *The American Political Science Review,* LII (September 1958), 725–744.

Jewell, Malcolm E. "Evaluating the Decline of Southern Internationalism through Senatorial Roll Call Votes," *Journal of Politics,* 21 (November 1959), 624–646.

Johnston, Bruce. "Farm Surpluses and Foreign Policy," *World Politics,* X (October 1957), 1–23.

Key, V. O. "The Politically Relevant in Surveys," *Public Opinion Quarterly,* XXIV (Spring 1960), 54–61.

Klingberg, Frank L. "The Historical Alternation of Moods in American Foreign Policy," *World Politics,* IV (January 1952), 239–273.

Lerche, Charles O. "Southern Congressmen and the 'New Isolationism,'" *Political Science Quarterly,* LXXV (September 1960), 321–337.

Mahanji, Usha. "Kennedy and the Strategy of Aid," *Western Political Quarterly,* XVIII (September 1965), 656–668.

Mallalieu, William C. "The Origins of the Marshall Plan," *Political Science Quarterly,* LXXIII (December 1958), 481–504.

Martin, Edwin M. "New Trends in United States Economic Foreign Policy," *The Annals,* 330 (July 1960), 67–76.

McCamy, James. "The Administration of Foreign Affairs in the United States," *World Politics,* VII (January 1955), 315–325.

McClosky, Herbert, *et al.* "Issue Conflict and Consensus among Party Leaders and Followers," *American Political Science Review,* LIV (June 1960), 406–427.

Miller, Warren, and Donald E. Stokes. "Constituency Influence in Congress," *The American Political Science Review,* LVII (March 1963), 45–56.

Morgenthau, Hans. "A Political Theory of Foreign Aid," *The*

American Political Science Review, LVI (June 1962), 301–309.

"No Wonder We're Broke," *U.S. News and World Report*, LII (April 23, 1962), 1.

Packenham, Robert. "Political Development Doctrines in the American Foreign Aid Program," *World Politics*, XVIII (January 1966), 194–235.

Public Opinion News Service. September 15, 1957.

Rieselbach, Leroy N. "The Basis of Isolationist Behavior," *Public Opinion Quarterly*, XXIV (Winter 1960), 645–657.

Rosenau, James N. Review of Bernard Cohen. *The Political Process. Public Opinion Quarterly*, XXI (Fall 1957), 398–399.

Russett, Bruce M. "Demography, Salience, and Isolationist Behavior," *Public Opinion Quarterly*, XXIV (Winter 1960), 658–664.

Schatz, Sayre P. "The American Approach to Foreign Aid and the Thesis of Low Absorptive Capacity," *The Quarterly Review of Economics and Business*, I (November 1961), 55–62.

Schelling, Thomas C. "American Foreign Assistance," *World Politics*, VII (July 1955), 606–639.

Stassen, Harold. "The Case for Private Investment Abroad," *Foreign Affairs*, 32 (April 1954), 402–415.

Stokes, Donald E. "Spatial Models of Party Competition," *The American Political Science Review*, LVII (June 1963), 368–377.

Turner, Julius. "Party and Constituency: Pressures on Congress," *The Johns Hopkins University Studies in Historical and Political Science*, LXIX (1951).

Viner, Jacob. "Economic Foreign Policy on the New Frontier," *Foreign Affairs*, 39 (July 1961), 560–577.

United States Government Publications

"AID Figures Illustrate U.S. Help to Alliance." AID Press Release, March 28, 1966.

The Brookings Institution, *The Administration of Foreign Affairs and Overseas Operations.* Washington, D.C.: U.S. GPO, June 1951.

Congressional Record, 1959–1962.

Cooperative-Democratic Institutions for Economic and Social Development. A Report by the Special Advisory Committee on Cooperatives to the Administrator of the Agency for International Development, November 1, 1961, processed.

Department of State Bulletin, 1948–1963.

Economic Assistance as a Cooperative Effort of the Free World, Department of State, n.d., processed.

Highlights of President Kennedy's New Act for International Development. Washington, D.C.: U.S. GPO, 1961.

Moscoso, Teodoro. "The Alliance for Progress," Washington, D.C.: Agency for International Development, n.d.

The Mutual Security Program for Fiscal Years 1952–1958. Washington, D.C.: U.S. GPO, 1951–1957.

Payments to U.S. Firms. Washington, D.C.: International Cooperation Administration, 1961.

Senate Committee on Interstate and Foreign Commerce. *Freedom of Communications: Pt. I and Pt. II,* 87th Cong. 1st Sess.

United States Department of State, *American Opinion Report,* 1950–1966.

Other Sources

Dexter, Lewis Anthony. *Congress and the People They Listen To.* Cambridge, Massachusetts: Center for International Studies, Massachusetts Institute of Technology, 1955, processed.

Eddy, Nancy Boardman. "Public Opinion and United States Foreign Policy, 1937–1956." America Project. Working Paper I, n.d., processed. Available from the Center for International Studies, Massachusetts Institute of Technology.

Foster, H. Schuyler. "Does Press Comment Represent Public Opinion?" No place of publication, May 15, 1953, processed.

Gibbons, William Conrad. "Political Action Analysis as an Approach to the Study of Congress and Foreign Policy." Unpublished Ph.D. dissertation, Princeton University, 1961.

Marvel, William Worthington. "Foreign Aid and United States Security." Unpublished Ph.D. dissertation, Princeton University, 1951.

Meet the Press, 5 (December 24, 1961).

Minnesota Poll on Foreign Aid. November 17, 1961, processed.

National Opinion Research Center. *American Programs of Foreign Aid,* February 1957, processed.

Pye, Lucian. "The Policy Implications of Social Change in Non-Western Societies." Cambridge, Mass.: Center for International Studies, Massachusetts Institute of Technology, April 1957, processed.

Raiford, William N. "Southern Congressmen and Foreign Aid." Unpublished Master's thesis, American University, 1962.

Rice, Andrew Eliot. "Building a Constituency for the Foreign Aid Program: The Record of the Eisenhower Years." Unpublished Ph.D. dissertation, Syracuse University, 1963.

Index

70
71
72
M
75
76
77
79
81
83
85
88